The Pre-K Home Companion

The Pre-K Home Companion

Learning the Importance of Early Childhood Education and Choosing the Best Program for Your Family

Sherelyn R. Kaufman, Michael J. Kaufman, and Elizabeth C. Nelson

ROWMAN & LITTLEFIELD
Lanham • Boulder • New York • London

Published by Rowman & Littlefield
A wholly owned subsidary of The Rowman & Littlefield Publishing Group, Inc.
4501 Forbes Boulevard, Suite 200, Lanham, Maryland 20706
www.rowman.com

Unit A, Whitacre Mews, 26-34 Stannary Street, London SE11 4AB

British Library Cataloguing in Publication Information Available

Library of Congress Cataloging-in-Publication Data

ISBN 978-1-4758-2157-4 (cloth : alk. paper) -- ISBN 978-1-4758-2159-8 (electronic)

♾ ™ The paper used in this publication meets the minimum requirements of American National Standard for Information Sciences Permanence of Paper for Printed Library Materials, ANSI/NISO Z39.48-1992.

Printed in the United States of America

To our grandparents, parents, and children
for making visible the joy of learning

Contents

Preface

This book is a one-stop resource for parents and families facing decisions about how to provide their children the best educational experiences before kindergarten. Will I enroll my child in an early learning program? Which centers are within our financial means? Which learning center's philosophy fits with my understanding of how young children learn? How will I know if my child is growing and learning? How will my child learn to solve problems?

In the spring of 2015, we published *Learning Together: The Law, Policy, Pedagogy, Economics, and Neuroscience of Early Childhood Education* (2015). In that book, we presented a wealth of research and evidence from across many disciplines, all of which demonstrates that an investment in early childhood education programs that encourage children to construct their knowledge through meaningful relationships would produce remarkable long-term academic, social, and economic benefits.

We also showed why families should strongly resist the temptation to enroll their children in an early childhood education program that markets a mistaken sense of kindergarten readiness, which is defined and measured by the short-term acquisition of shallow academic skills. Rather, early childhood education programs that encourage children to construct their knowledge through meaningful relationships produce the greatest long-term success and well-being.

We are grateful for the positive response to our book. That response has inspired us to write this new book, designed to help families make critically important decisions about the best early learning environments for their children.

In this book, we recognize that early childhood learning experiences have a dramatic impact on the success and well-being of children, the community, and the country. Children who have positive early childhood experiences develop cognitive and socio-emotional abilities that lead to positive school performance, income, family stability, and health. This in turn produces particularly robust educational, social, and economic benefits for children and for the country.

Government and community leaders have recognized the importance of early childhood programs. The landscape of early childhood opportunities is shifting rapidly. The national, state, and local governments are focusing like never before on the value of improving access to early childhood education opportunities for all families.

The movement toward universal access to pre-K education is growing. In cities such as New York and San Antonio, and in states such as Oklahoma, for example, virtually all four-year-olds are now being offered access to early childhood education.

With the spread of access and opportunities comes a dramatic increase in the choices available to families in educating their young children. Parents seek "quality" services, and yet are offered little guidance as to what this means. They hear a lot of uninformed buzz about the importance of "kindergarten readiness," but they really want to know which kind of programs will best prepare their children not just for the next year, but for the next one hundred years.

We trust families to make wise decisions once they have gathered the necessary information. We provide the information. This companion offers background on why early childhood education is important in your child's life. It provides an overview of current research about how young children learn. We suggest questions that families may ask potential service providers about a program's policies and practices. And we hope to spark dialogue among family members, immediate and extended, about what qualities in a pre-K environment are most important to a child's development.

A companion makes a journey more enriching, while providing support and perspective. We hope that this book will be helpful to parents as they make vital decisions about the welfare of their children, and their community.

Acknowledgments

The authors first thank the foremost scholars, leaders, and practitioners in the field of early childhood education who offered invaluable suggestions to improve prior drafts of our work, including W. Steven Barnett, Joan Bradbury, Cathy Fishbain Brown, Carolyn Edwards, Angela Fowler, Lella Gandini, Rachel Gubman, Maureen Hager, Kassandra Hayes, Rebekah F. Kaufman, David Kirp, Dolores Kohl, Basak Notz, Susan Ochshorn, Erica Oehler, James Ryan, Heidi Stevens, Dana Suskind, and Lynn White.

We also thank the extraordinary educators who inspired this book, particularly Rose Alschuler, Norman Amaker, George Anastaplo, Nina S. Appel, Jennifer Avery-Imani, Carol Aymar, Dan Baltierra, Mary Bell, Svetlana Budilovsky, Marcus Campbell, James P. Carey, Patricia F. Carini, Margie Carter, Carter Cast, Harry Clor, Maureen Condon, Richard Conviser, Margie Cooper, Barbara Cross, Deb Curtis, Johanna Davis, John Dewey, Meredith Dodd, Amelia Gambetti, Howard Gardner, Diane Geraghty, Jacqueline Griesdorn, Tommy Grogan, David Hawkins, Frances Hawkins, James Hayes, Jeremiah Howe, Alise Shafer Ivey, Brittny Lissner Johnson, Daniel Kahneman, Judy Kaminsky, Alfie Kohn, Mary Korte, Michelle Korte, Jody Lapp, Kirk LaRue, Rachel Lee, Richard Louv, Lisa Makoul, Loris Malaguzzi, Mary Ann Manley, Cindy McPherson, Nanci Moore, Martin Moran, Pam Myers, Lisa Nielsen, Dana O'Brien, Honi Papernik, Trish Parenti, Francis W. Parker, Ann Pelo, Neil Postman, Alan Raphael, Carlina Rinaldi, Javier Rivera, Susan Rooney, Peter Rutkoff, William Shapiro, Ronald Sharp, Daniel Siegel, Ashleigh St. Peters, Lonnie Stonitsch, Liza Sullivan, Kimeri Swanson-Beck, Priscilla Taylor, Liz Tertel, Cathy Topal, Paul Tough, Vea Vecchi, Merrilee Waldron, Carleton Washburne, Lynn White, Carolyn Wing, and David Yellen.

We thank as well for their wisdom and guidance regarding education law and policy: United States Department of Education, Office for Civil Rights, directors and attorneys, especially Kenneth A. Mines and John Fry; elected school board members and public servants, Rebecca Baim, Joan Herczeg, Debbie Hymen, Michael Lipsitz, Jerrold Marks, and Terri Olian; school district administrators, Trisha Kocanda, Gregory M. Kurr, and Michael Lubelfeld; and school lawyers, Nancy Krent, Mike Loizzi, Bob Kohn, Heather Brickman, John A. Relias, and James C. Franczek Jr.

Thanks also to the caring and dedicated colleagues we have encountered from early childhood education to law and graduate school: the Ravinia Nursery School leaders and staff, including Marilyn Straus, Rosalie Weinfeld, Ruth Stern, Rosalie Edelstein, Midge Hechtman, Ginger Scott, Ginger Uhlmann, and Roberta Wexler; the elementary school professionals and middle school educators who opened our eyes to what a "good" school could be; the "teachers' teachers" at National-Louis University and Baker Demonstration School in Evanston, Illinois, especially Paula Jorde Bloom, Marge Leon, Kathleen McKenna, Cynthia Mee, Alan Rossman, and Jane Stenson; the students, faculty, and administrators of Erikson Institute, particularly Stephanie Bynum, Rhonda Gillis, and Gillian Dowley McNamee; the wonderful teachers, board members, and families of Winnetka Public School Nursery; and the visionary early childhood education experts of Family Network and the Community Family Center, particularly Barbara Haley, William S. Kaufman, and Herbert S. Wander.

Thank you to the extraordinary learning community of Francis W. Parker School, parents, children, and professionals alike. And we extend our sincere gratitude to Linda McLaren at Northwestern University Settlement House Head Start and to Jean Wallace Baker and Lisa Adelmund at Highland Park Community Nursery School, for demonstrating what unfailing dedication to young children, their families, and communities looks like.

For their invaluable research, editorial assistance, and feedback on early drafts of the book, we also are grateful to an outstanding group of Loyola University of Chicago law students and Graduate Fellows, including Sean Langan and John Wunderlich. We thank all of the parents who offered candid feedback on drafts of this book to ensure that it was a true companion for their peers, especially Kristin Mann, Katie Kaul, and Holly Schumaker.

In addition, the authors wish to thank the outstanding team at Rowman & Littlefield for their tremendous support and assistance throughout this project, particularly Thomas Koerner and Carlie Wall.

Introduction: How Can This Book Be a Helpful Companion?

The child has a hundred languages . . .
—Loris Malaguzzi

This book is the only resource you need as you begin your search for the best early childhood education program for your child.

Part I helps you navigate the various programs available in your community. In this section, we offer guidance on major factors that you need to consider:

- cost
- philosophy
- discipline
- technology
- special education services
- dual-language learning
- diversity
- accreditation
- additional practical concerns

Although you are the one who must decide how to weigh these critical factors, this Companion will show that families should resist the temptation to enroll their children in early childhood education programs that tout a narrow and short-sighted sense of "kindergarten readiness." Such programs often try to convince families of their value by claiming that they quickly prepare children to perform traditional academic skills that are measured on standardized tests.

But as we show throughout this book, the evidence demonstrates that the early childhood education programs that foster the greatest long-term success and well-being for children are those that develop critical relationship-building competencies such as listening, communicating, collaborating, negotiating, persevering, and perspective taking. Such programs: (1) are affordable; (2) follow a social constructivist approach, which prioritizes these critical relationship-building skills; (3) adhere to developmentally appropriate discipline policies based on the model of restorative justice; (4) use technology only as one of many materials to support learning relationships; (5) provide a fully inclusive and supportive environment for children with special needs; (6) embrace children for whom English is an additional language; and (7) foster a diverse learning community.

This first section also will help you to navigate various accreditation and learning standards, as well as practical considerations to weigh when selecting a program, including schedule, location, and convenience.

Once you know what to consider when making your choice, we help you to make the choice. Part I concludes by giving you strategies for pursuing Internet research, engaging with other members of your community, gathering materials from various schools, and visiting the school and school administrators.

This Companion also recognizes that choosing a school is just the beginning of your child's learning experience. Accordingly, we next discuss how to build meaningful relationships with the school and with the community as a whole, because it is through meaningful relationships that your child learns and you learn to support that learning. Part II helps you to support your child by strengthening relationships between school and home. It shows families how to bring home and to the upper grades the same kind of relationship-based learning that takes place in an effective early childhood education program. And we give you ways to know whether and how your child is learning.

Finally, Part III provides to families, teachers, and administrators at all levels, as well as policymakers, methods of building meaningful relationships throughout the community surrounding the school. We offer suggestions on how you can help your child develop as a citizen with the power to improve the world, and we conclude by offering suggestions on how you can help all children have greater access to critical early childhood education opportunities.

Throughout this Companion, we provide you with information based on experience, best practices, and a wealth of research and evidence from a variety of disciplines. Each of our points has support in authorities referenced at the end of the book. If you would like more detailed citations precisely linked to each separate statement, we also invite you to consult *Learning Together* and the footnotes throughout that book.

Part I

How Do I Choose the Best Early Childhood Education Program for My Family?

Part I discusses why early childhood programs are so important and sets forth the major factors you should consider when choosing an early childhood education program for your child, including: (1) cost; (2) educational philosophy; (3) discipline; (4) technology; (5) special education services; (6) dual language; (7) diversity; (8) accreditation; and (9) additional practical concerns. It also provides strategies for researching and choosing an early childhood education program that is right for your family.

Chapter One

Why Is Early Childhood Education Important?

The first years last forever.
—Rob Reiner

You may be wondering whether to enroll your child in an early childhood program. Many parents feel that the home environment is best suited to their child's early development. Others may feel that a center-based program represents an intrusion into the private life of the family. Indeed, the number of families who decide to homeschool their children has grown over the past two decades. Parents who decide to homeschool their children decide for a variety of reasons, including religious beliefs and safety concerns. Currently, almost 2 percent of children of school age are homeschooled.

Many families, however, feel that they cannot teach their young children in the home. Their work schedules or other responsibilities simply do not permit them to do so. And many of those with the means to choose homeschooling understand that center-based early childhood education programs do not replace the learning that takes place in the home. Rather, they are an indispensable supplement to a nurturing home environment.

The evidence is clear: A child's early learning environment is critical to that child's success and well-being. Thanks to recent path-breaking research into the importance of early childhood education programs, we now know that:

1. Cognitive abilities and socio-emotional skills, physical and mental health, perseverance, attention, motivation, and self-confidence are important determinants of success.

2. Children who experience an effective early learning environment before kindergarten develop cognitive and socio-emotional abilities—these very skills that are such important determinants of success—that lead to positive school performance, income, family stability, and health.
3. Children who do not experience an effective early learning environment before kindergarten, conversely, are more likely to have negative school performance, special education needs, behavioral problems, grade retention, criminal involvement, imprisonment, ill health, unstable family life, and diminished economic success.
4. High-quality early childhood programs foster cognitive and socio-emotional abilities in young children that produce long-term success and well-being.

In particular, children who received the benefits of high-quality preschool programming dramatically outperformed those who did not:

1. *High school completion*: Some 77 percent received a high school diploma or general education development (GED) diploma, compared to 60 percent.
2. *Employment*: Some 69 percent were employed at age twenty-seven, compared to 56 percent; 76 percent were employed at age forty, compared to 62 percent.
3. *Income*: Those treatment-group students who were employed at age twenty-seven had higher earnings (by $2,000 each) than those control-group students who were employed; those treatment-group students who were employed at age forty had higher earnings (by $5,500 each) than those control-group students who were employed.
4. *Home ownership*: Some 27 percent owned their homes at age twenty-two, compared to 5 percent; 37 percent owned their homes at age forty, compared to 28 percent.
5. *Arrest and prison record*: Some 36 percent were arrested five or more times, compared to 55 percent; 28 percent were imprisoned, compared to 52 percent.
6. *School engagement*: Some 67 percent were prepared for elementary school, compared to 28 percent.
7. *Educational achievement*: Some 49 percent were achieving at grade level at age fourteen, compared to 15 percent.

More than 150 scientific studies have been examined and reexamined, analyzed and meta-analyzed. Every one of these studies demonstrates that an investment in early childhood education produces substantial long-term educational, social, and economic benefits for all children, regardless of socioeconomic status, race, or ethnicity.

And yet many three- and four-year-olds are currently not enrolled in an early childhood education program. There are approximately four million four-year-olds in America, and a similar number of three-year-olds. Of three-year-olds, 60 percent are not enrolled in a program, and of four-year-olds, 25 percent are not enrolled in a program.

The millions of children left out tend to be from relatively poor and less-educated families. The enrollment of children from low-income families in which parents have not completed high school is far below average. Middle-income families have relatively low participation rates, and the enrollment of children from upper-income households in which parents have graduate degrees is far above average. Latino and Hispanic children tend to have very low enrollment rates, and African American children have high enrollment rates but the least access to programs deemed to be of high quality.

In 2011, higher percentages of three-to-five-year-olds whose parents had either a graduate or professional degree (75 percent) or a bachelor's degree (71 percent) were enrolled in early childhood education programs than children of parents with any other levels of educational attainment. Some 53 percent of children whose parents had less than a high school degree and 58 percent of children whose parents completed high school were enrolled in early childhood education programs.

Accordingly, there is a significant disparity in access to effective early childhood education programs based upon race, ethnicity, and socioeconomic status. That disparity harms everyone. In the pages that follow, we offer families information that will empower them to advocate for early childhood programs that are not only accessible but also use professional educators who use best educational practices. We hope that when families demand more of these programs, the supply will grow to meet the increasing demand. In our final chapter, we also encourage families to pursue a host of strategies to encourage policymakers to increase access to effective early childhood education programs for all children.

Chapter Two

Which Options Are Affordable for My Family?

Education is not preparation for life; education is life itself.
—John Dewey

Cost is often a determinative factor in making the decision about where to send your child to pre-K. You may find a tremendous disparity in the cost of early childhood education programs.

Early childhood education programs are publicly funded, privately funded, or some combination of the two. The great bulk of money used to support publicly funded early childhood programs comes from state and local governments, as is true of education funding generally. This is, quite simply, our tax dollars at work. Public financial support for early childhood education derives from federal Head Start funds, federal special education funds from the Individuals with Disabilities Education Act, and state and local educational funds.

Prices for private programs vary dramatically. As such, it may be helpful to identify both public and private options available in your community and to look into whether you qualify for state or federal funded programs. Some programs charge based on a sliding scale determined by your annual income.

When trying to determine what types of early childhood programs are available in your area, asking around by word of mouth, looking at flyers in local libraries, doing Internet research, and visiting local school websites or the schools themselves may provide some insight into the types of subsidized programs available to you in your geographic area and give you a general sense of cost.

Some programs, such as cooperative schools, may be very low cost but require substantial parent involvement. Still other programs may be very costly, costing tens of thousands of dollars each year.

When researching the cost of each program, determine whether the school charges on a semester, monthly, or installment basis. Schools that bill on a semester basis generally require two payments each year, one in the fall and one in the winter. Other schools may require a family pay each month or a certain number of times each year. Once you've determined how your school charges tuition, research whether there are any additional fees such as program, enrollment, or supply fees you are required to pay. If cost is a barrier for you, inquire directly with the program's director about scholarship opportunities. Nothing ventured, nothing gained.

Some employers subsidize an employee's childcare expenses, including early childhood education programs. There are two possible advantages to these subsidies: (1) the employer often defrays the cost of the care; and (2) the employee's remaining costs are subtracted from wages and are not taxed as income. These programs are often known as Dependent Care Flexible Spending Accounts and can provide substantial savings to working individuals of all income levels.

The cost of a program is not always related to its quality; hence, once you have determined your budget, this is but one of many factors you should consider when deciding where to send your child. The sections below detail the different ways to fund pre-K.

A. OPTION 1: STATE-FUNDED PRE-K PROGRAMS

The first way to pay for early childhood education programs is to locate a state-funded pre-K program. There are fifty-two state-funded early childhood education programs in forty states. Hawaii, Idaho, Indiana, Mississippi, Montana, New Hampshire, North Dakota, South Dakota, Utah, and Wyoming do not have state-funded early childhood education programs.

Publicly funded programs are designed to substantially increase access to early childhood programs to families with the lowest income. The state subsidizes these programs, which allows eligible families to enroll at no cost, or at a deep discount.

B. OPTION 2: FEDERALLY FUNDED HEAD START PROGRAMS

The largest federal early childhood program in the United States is Head Start, a U.S. Department of Health and Human Services program. Established in 1965 as a key part of the nation's War on Poverty, the federal Head Start program provides early learning programs for children in impoverished families. Head Start promotes educational development for children in these families by offering educational, nutritional, health, social, and other services.

While the Office of Head Start, a part of the U.S. Department of Health and Human Services, administers Head Start federally, Head Start programs are operated by local school districts, other local governmental agencies, or private organizations that receive a five-year renewable grant from the federal government. Local programs are operated through grants to public agencies, private nonprofit organizations, faith-based organizations, and school systems.

Because they are locally operated, Head Start programs vary significantly from one to the next. In 2014, 1,622 organizations received Head Start grants to provide early childhood education, 1,016 of which were local school districts. Most Head Start programs operate a part-day program, but they are sometimes coordinated with state funds to provide families with an affordable full-day program.

If you seek services for a child under four years of age, an Early Head Start program may be best for you. The Early Head Start program is designed to support low-income families and their children from birth to age three. The program provides home visits and center-based services, including prenatal and postnatal counseling, nutritional advice, and support for early childhood health and development.

1. Is My Child Eligible for Head Start?

Head Start eligibility depends on family income. A family that earns under the amount listed in the Federal Poverty Guidelines (FPG) is automatically eligible to send their child to Head Start. The number of people in a family or household determines the exact cutoff for eligibility. For example, a family of four that earns up to $24,250 is within the FPG. Likewise, a family of five that earns up to $28,410 is within the FPG. Therefore, if your family income is less than this number, you automatically qualify for Head Start.

Although Head Start is primarily meant for children from families within the FPG, providers may also serve children from families earning more than the amount listed in the FPG. The Head Start Act allows providers to give up to 10 percent of their seats to children who would benefit from the program regardless of what their family earns. It also allows providers to open up to 35 percent of their seats to children from families earning more than the amount listed in the FPG, but below 130 percent (or 1.3 times the size) of that amount. To illustrate, a family of four earning $31,525 a year (1.3 times the FPG "cutoff" of $28,410) could still send their child to Head Start. This opens Head Start to many families who, despite earning an amount greater than the FPG, would still be hard-pressed to finance their child's preschool education by themselves.

Local Head Start providers must first show that they prioritize and effectively serve children from households within the FPG. In fact, providers must try to fill all available spots with these children before offering seats to children from relatively more affluent households. Any Head Start provider that serves children from the "130 percent" category is subject to a yearly review of its policies. Families slightly beyond the FPG cutoff should realize that their chances of participating in Head Start might change from year to year, and their children are not automatically eligible.

Certain groups of children are automatically eligible for Head Start regardless of their family's income. These include children in foster care, homeless children, and children from families receiving assistance through Supplemental Security Income (SSI) or Temporary Assistance for Needy Families (TANF). Children from families receiving assistance through other federal programs—including Disability Insurance—are not automatically eligible for Head Start.

2. What Is Head Start's Approach?

Head Start programs take a comprehensive approach to early childhood education, including health services, nutrition, wellness, parent education, and social services. In recent years the federal Department of Health and Human Services has promulgated Head Start "performance standards" that emphasize academic achievement, particularly traditional literacy skills.

Specifically, Head Start Program Performance Standards require that children: (1) develop print and numeracy awareness; (2) understand and use an increasingly complex and varied vocabulary; (3) develop and demonstrate an appreciation of books; and, for non-English-speaking children: (4) that English-language learners progress toward acquisition of the English language.

Head Start's learning outcomes require that children know that letters of the alphabet are a special category of visual graphics and that words are units of print. They also require that children be able to identify at least ten letters of the alphabet and associate sounds with written words.

In order to achieve these goals, Head Start created a set of objectives focused on the development and learning outcomes of low-income children. Local Head Start programs are given a good deal of flexibility to select or design and implement a developmentally appropriate curriculum consistent with children's interests, temperaments, and backgrounds. Head Start strives to balance child-initiated and adult-directed activities, including individual and small-group activities, in the daily program. There are certain earmarks of a Head Start program:

- Supporting social and emotional development by building trust; fostering independence; encouraging self-control by setting clear, consistent limits and having realistic expectations; encouraging respect for the feelings and rights of others; and providing timely, predictable, and unrushed routines and transitions.
- Each child's learning is to be supported through experimentation, inquiry, observation, play, exploration, and related strategies. Art, music, movement, and dialogue are viewed as key opportunities for creative self-expression, and language use among children and between children and adults is promoted. Developmentally appropriate activities and materials are to be provided for support of children's emerging literacy and numeracy development.
- Center-based programs are to provide sufficient time, space, equipment, materials, and adult guidance for active play and movement that supports fine and gross motor development. Provisions and encouragement for social and symbolic forms of play help young children's self-regulation and social competence. Home-based programs are to encourage parents to appreciate the value of physical development and to provide opportunities for safe and active play.

The impact of Head Start is difficult to measure because of the variety of programs and the inadequacy and unevenness of funding. You may have heard some people argue that the benefits of Head Start fade by the time a child reaches second or third grade. But those voices are misleading. The best evidence shows significant positive differences in long-term outcomes between children who had access to Head Start and those in the control group who did not have such access. Moreover, results of the large-scale Head Start Impact Study indicate that Head Start had positive impacts on several aspects of children's development during their time in the program.

3. Will Head Start Meet My Child's Special Developmental Needs?

Head Start providers must now reserve at least 10 percent of their seats for children with "developmental delays." Each state determines for itself what counts as a "developmental delay," meaning eligibility standards are not the same across the country. In addition, Head Start providers must offer early intervention services for children who are considered "at risk" for delayed development.

Developmental delays that you may seek services for may fall into any one of five categories. These categories are: (1) physical development, (2) cognitive development, (3) communication development, (4) social or emotional development, and (5) adaptive development (self-sufficiency).

Federal law also provides for many services designed to help children with developmental delays thrive. These include measures ranging from home visits and family counseling to psychological treatment and physical therapy. Federal law requires that children receiving special assistance not be separated from their classmates unless it is absolutely necessary. This reinforces to both the child and family that they are valued members of the learning community.

4. Where Can I Apply for Head Start?

If you believe you are eligible for a state or federal program, you should begin by using the Head Start Locator on the Office of the Administration for Children and Families Early Childhood Learning & Knowledge Center (ECLKC) at https://eclkc.ohs.acf.hhs.gov/hslc. Then call the phone number listed for a Head Start program near your home.

Since Head Start awards grants to so many different providers, parents may find it difficult to obtain the information they need. Head Start's presence in Chicago, Illinois, illustrates this confusion. Although Chicago Public School (CPS) receives a large block grant, it distributes the money among many other service providers. Between this and other grants, roughly 480 Head Start providers operate in Chicago. To obtain specific, practical information, parents should contact the local providers directly.

Local Head Start providers handle all applications and forms, and specific practices may vary slightly. Parents should remember that all local providers must follow federal policies and cannot make many independent decisions. Admissions policies, for example, are quite rigid—in other words, a provider is not free to open up 45 percent of its slots to children from families earning more than the FPG instead of the required 35 percent of slots.

Although filling out a Head Start application form can seem intimidating, you should take comfort in knowing that providers will assist parents and walk them through the form. You can expect to answer questions about your family circumstances and income, as well as your child's medical history and educational needs. In addition to English, forms are available in languages common to particular areas. For example, Miami-Dade County, Florida, offers applications in Spanish and Creole.

C. OPTION 3: FEDERALLY FUNDED SPECIAL EDUCATION PROGRAMS

If your child is determined to be eligible for special education services, the federal government may support the cost of your child's education under a law known as the Individuals with Disabilities Education Improvement Act (IDEA).

In chapter 7, we help you to navigate the process by which your child may become eligible for special education services. But even if your child is determined to be eligible, it is important to recognize that the total amount of available governmental funds will likely fall short of providing adequate funding. While it is true that school districts spend about 1.9 times more to educate a child with special needs than they do to educate other children, this amount still does not come close to reaching what is necessary to provide an adequate education.

For you as a parent, this means that your child or other children in your community may be attending programs that are not fully funded. There is no question that funding matters. If a program is not fully funded, that means that your program may not have enough money to provide your child even the level of minimal educational services that is required by law. For example, a lack of full funding could deprive your child of the kind of one-on-one support or assistive technology that enables that child to communicate with their teachers or peers, to develop meaningful relationships, and to learn and grow. Once your child is determined eligible for special education services, you may need to become a strong advocate to be sure that adequate and appropriate services are provided.

D. OPTION 4: PRIVATE AND RELIGIOUS PROGRAMS

Another way to pay for early childhood programs is, of course, to pay out of pocket for a private or religious program. There are many outstanding private and religious-affiliated programs throughout the country. Approximately 18 percent of three-year-olds and 34 percent of four-year-olds attend these private early childhood education programs.

Private programs vary dramatically in their cost. Cooperative schools, where parents regularly assist the teacher on a rotating basis, often are more affordable than schools that are not cooperative. In-home private care can be a viable alternative for families in neighborhoods where that option is available. As with any early childhood education opportunity, families should look for evidence that a home care facility meets all accrediting standards for quality and safety. These standards are detailed in chapter 10.

Programs operated under the auspices of a religious organization are often housed in religious facilities. It is not unusual for the true cost of attendance to be subsidized by the religious organization, perhaps by the organization providing the center with lower-than-market-rate rent. Some private early childhood programs are housed in religious facilities but have no religious affiliation. They offer services to a parent population for a weekly, monthly, or annual fee. Some of these private programs operate for a profit. Many are not-for-profit organizations. Scholarships may be available, and you risk nothing by inquiring. In addition, schools that serve pre-K through middle or high school often charge high tuitions for pre-K. In this instance, you may be paying for routine or guaranteed acceptance into that school's kindergarten program.

Some popular private programs operate for a profit. Tuition costs can reach as high as $35,000 per year. Parents who can afford those high costs may be tempted to believe that these high costs are an indication of quality. Parents should resist that temptation. Many such programs "sell" their ability to make a child "kindergarten ready," or dazzle with fancy facilities and elaborate technology. As we discuss in chapter 12, a parent should not be distracted by these bells and whistles. The true indication of value is an environment in which respected educators encourage children and adults to build meaningful relationships. Such an environment creates genuine "readiness," not just for kindergarten, but for life. It need not be expensive.

E. OPTION 5: PUBLIC-PRIVATE PARTNERSHIPS AND SLIDING-SCALE FUNDING

Several states and districts have established public-private partnerships to fund early childhood education programs. In a public-private partnership, a government agency enters into an agreement with a private sector organization to provide a public service.

In the context of early childhood education, a school district may contribute to a private provider financial support, certified teachers, training, professional development, materials, supplies, and equipment. A school district may have resources that can enhance program delivery. Additionally, a school district may be able to provide to a private provider guidance on personnel, payroll, and policy decisions, and administrative functions. The private provider may contribute space, "wrap-around care," advertising to the community, wellness screenings, and additional resources.

One example of a public/private partnership is Educare. This national early childhood education program is open full day and full year and serves at-risk children from birth to five years old. Funds for the program are provided from multiple sources—Head Start, Early Head Start, the Child Care Block Grant, and state pre-K funds—along with private funds to support Educare's delivery of a high quality program. Anchor philanthropists, foundations, the local school districts, and other local and community partners support Educare facilities. In Educare learning environments, children receive an array of early childhood services—everything the research suggests is effective—under one roof.

You may need to ask your local school district if there is an early childhood public/private partnership active in your community. And if the answer is no, you may want to bring the idea to your local school board or other elected representatives.

Chapter Three

How Do I Choose among Various Pedagogical Approaches to Early Childhood Education?

Education is the kindling of a flame, not the filling of a vessel.
—Socrates

Once you have decided whether your child should attend a public program, a private program, or a blended public-private program, the next step is to determine which approach to pre-K education is best for your child.

Early childhood education programs offer a wide range of educational approaches. Some approaches emphasize social and emotional development, while others prioritize short-term academic performance. In this chapter, the book presents a continuum of pedagogical approaches, from those that tend to use direct instruction of traditional academic skills to those that emphasize social constructivist practices. The chapter will set forth the philosophy, methods, and goals of each approach so that parents and families can make an informed choice about which approach is best for their child.

These distinctions are somewhat artificial. Many outstanding early childhood programs use a variety of these approaches. While some programs along this continuum use a canned, preset curriculum, others provide to highly skilled educators the professional training and the discretion to interweave a variety of these approaches to meet the particular, emergent interests and needs of their students.

A. DIRECT INSTRUCTION OF TRADITIONAL ACADEMIC SKILLS

The direct instruction approach prioritizes the development of traditional academic skills, particularly those characterized as literacy and math. In these classrooms, the teacher often functions as the authoritarian figure while the students are expected to be consumers of information.

The direct instruction approach is founded on behaviorism, or the belief that learning is defined as a change in observable behavior. In this approach, the role of the teacher is to provide direct instruction of information and to use positive and negative reinforcements to reward or punish student conduct. The teacher is often the dominant source of information to the students, primarily through lecture. To reinforce certain behavior, teachers provide particular pieces of information in a sequential order and present their instruction in a linear way so that they can ensure that one particular desired behavior is observed before proceeding to the next.

Under this traditional academic method, there is often an emphasis on testing, predetermined curricula, and standardized assessments to measure student outcomes. In a culture that places value on learning and testing these academic skills, some parents and families may be led to believe an early childhood environment that focuses on learning the alphabet and numbers may be optimal.

The evidence, however, indicates that too much time spent on direct instruction of traditional academic skills does young children a disservice. While children can and should be learning literacy and math skills in pre-K, the way in which they learn these skills can vary from one environment to the next. In an environment that relies heavily on direct instruction, children may have a "letter of the week" or curriculum that sets goals as to how many letters or numbers a child recognizes. They may be able to consume the information and repeat it in a rote manner in a standardized testing format.

Parents may find some short-term comfort in their child's ability to perform well on a snapshot test. But if this method of instruction dominates the early childhood education environment, children may be denied the opportunity to develop the kind of meaningful relationships from which lasting knowledge and life-long well-being emerge.

B. THE CONSTRUCTIVIST APPROACH

1. The Foundations of the Constructivist Approach

The foundation of the constructivist program is that children learn by constructing knowledge, rather than receiving it through direct instruction. Jean Piaget was among the first to demonstrate this by recognizing that thought is constructed within each individual child's mind, and then the child develops language to repeat that thought to others. In constructivist programs, children construct knowledge individually with the teacher as a supervisor rather than an authoritarian figure.

2. An Example of the Constructivist Approach: Montessori-Inspired Programs

In 1907, Maria Montessori, a physician and anthropologist, created a program for low-income children in Rome. In this program, educators enabled children to construct their own knowledge through involvement in the practical experiences necessary for everyday life.

In a Montessori program, the child is a constant inquirer who interacts purposefully and actively within a carefully designed environment. The Montessori environment is to be ordered, proportioned to the child's size, and aesthetically pleasing. The environment should invite, support, and make possible learning. The teacher's job is to observe and manage each child's development.

For Montessori, there are six essential components of a constructivist learning environment: (1) freedom, (2) structure, (3) reality, (4) the natural world, (5) specific materials, and (6) productive sociability:

- *Freedom*: Montessori believed that the natural thrust of children is toward independence, and educators should follow the child's lead. Accordingly, children may choose among the materials and experiences offered. Where a child takes on a task, attention is fixed on that task to strengthen the child's focus and self-discipline. In this sense, a child's learning is individualistic and self-directed.
- *A Structured Environment*: Montessori believed that the external environment should promote the internal organization within the child. Rhythms and routines should be predictable, materials should be organized, and delivery of lessons should be precise.
- *Reality*: Montessori felt strongly that young children should be immersed in a world of reality rather than fantasy because real-world experiences develop the child's imagination. Children should work with authentic materials such as brooms and glassware that tangibly represent the real world.
- *The Natural World*: Similarly, Montessori felt that nature should be part of the learning experience because children are inherently drawn to it. Many Montessori classrooms have plants, animals, and small gardens that the children care for.
- *Materials*: In a Montessori learning environment, materials progress from simple to complex. When a child masters a skill, that child may then move on to an activity that requires more steps or more complex thinking.

- *Productive Sociability*: In a Montessori classroom, children may interact with each other to assist their productivity rather than to merely socialize.

The Montessori program is generally divided into practical life, sensorial, language, and mathematics.

- Practical life includes home-based activities that involve self-care, care of the environment, life skills, fine-motor development, and community living. Children, for example, may be taught to spoon, to pour, and then to cook.
- Sensorial refers to the fact that children are immersed in a stimulus-rich environment and are therefore given a series of sequenced exercises and materials so as to classify and sharpen their sensory impressions. As the child progresses through the series, the child refines his or her judgment and perception.
- Language development is fostered through the environment, where specific materials are introduced to promote language and literacy development. In order to learn to write, for example, the child must first acquire the mechanics of writing by tracing and drawing and handling individual wooden letters.
- Mathematics is rooted in the order, precision, and sequencing skills fostered through practical life and the Montessori materials. A child, for example, thus explores spatial relations through making patterns and temporal relationships through experiencing the daily routine.

Contemporary Montessori programs also emphasize child self-expression through the visual arts, music, dance, and drama.

Because Montessori-inspired programs encourage children to construct their own knowledge under the supervision of professional educators, these programs have significant advantages over those that emphasize direct instruction. Today, many Montessori-inspired programs also include elements of the social constructivist approach.

C. THE SOCIAL CONSTRUCTIVIST APPROACH

1. The Foundations of the Social Constructivist Approach

In social constructivist programs, the role of the teacher is to be a partner in learning with the student, who is a designer, builder, and inventor. The core tenet of social constructivist programs is to build knowledge through meaningful relationships.

Programs built on social constructivist principles often identify themselves as being "play based." These play-based programs are sometimes distinguished from academic programs. But the distinction between play and the development of academic skills is a false one. What you need to remember is that play is the vehicle through which your child experiences meaningful social interactions and, with appropriate guidance and support, develops important academic skills.

In the best play-based programs, educators practice social constructivist methods. They outfit the environment to inspire free play and exploration, while observing and interacting to encourage individual and community growth. This latter activity can be described as "guided play."

When the movement between free play (emerging from children's interests) and guided play (emerging when a skilled educator interacts in developmentally appropriate ways with children to stretch or deepen their thinking) is fluid, meaningful learning takes place. Accordingly, such play-based programs have been proven to produce greater academic achievement than any other method of early childhood education, including pure direct instruction.

Lev Vygotsky, a Russian child psychologist whose work was discovered after his death, proved that children construct their knowledge primarily through social interactions, thereby demonstrating that guided play is indispensible to all learning. Significantly, Vygotsky provided evidence showing what many parents know: a child's mental processes grow in an exchange among human beings. Without a shared, social experience, knowledge cannot be constructed.

The child's social context, which is an integral part of the very process of thinking and learning, also includes the child's family, school, culture, and society. All of these social networks are not merely received by a child; they shape the way in which the child thinks.

As a consequence, a child's thoughts also are bound up with the multiple languages in which the child shares his or her experiences with others. Because knowledge is constructed in social relationships, knowledge is dependent upon communication. A child thinks only by communicating with others.

Based upon Vygotsky's work, the step-by-step process by which your child constructs knowledge can be mapped as follows:

1. Your child is naturally driven toward meaningful social relationships.
2. Your child encounters meaningful social relationships.
3. Your child naturally desires to share his or her experiences with others in that meaningful social relationship.
4. Your child naturally seeks to represent to others his or her perceptions.
5. Your child develops multiple languages to communicate perceptions to others.

6. Your child develops the mental process used to communicate successfully his or her experience to others, including the mental process
   required to receive input from others.
7. Your child develops the mental process necessary to replicate the
   communications.
8. Your child internalizes the shared experience and the mental process
   by communicating the experience to himself or herself within the
   child's own mind.
9. Your child's mind has been reshaped and strengthened by the experience.
10. Your child has constructed language.
11. Your child has constructed knowledge.

Vygotsky's research has profound implications for early learning environments. Based on his work, we know that:

- *Teachers and Children Co-Construct Knowledge*: Vygotsky believed that
  children construct their own understandings in conjunction with the teacher rather than passively reproducing whatever is presented to them.
- *Scaffolding Helps Children Make a Transition to Independence*: For most
  children, the transition from assisted to independent learning is gradual
  and involves using a great deal of assistance before no assistance is
  needed. This means the teacher must scaffold or support student learning
  by first designing and then following a plan for providing and withdraw-
  ing assistance over time.
- *Instruction Should Amplify Child Development, Not Accelerate It*: Vygotsky's students condemned the idea of accelerating development. Instead, a
  teacher must work with the child within the child's "zone of proximal
  development" or ZPD—the place where the child makes progress toward
  being able to develop new capacities that the child can engage in without
  adult assistance. By working with the child within the ZPD, the teacher
  helps the child to grow to be able to use skills independently.
- *Play Is the Foundation for Learning*: Vygotsky's definition of play is
  limited to dramatic or make-believe play. "Real" play consists of: (1)
  children creating an imaginary situation; (2) children taking on and acting
  out roles; and (3) children following a set of rules determined by specific
  roles. For Vygotsky, mastery of academic skills is not as good a predictor
  of children's scholastic abilities as the quality of their play.

Play is valuable for child development in part because it develops the
following competencies that make children ready for formal schooling:

- *Self-Regulation*: Play helps children develop the ability to self-regulate their behaviors rather than acting on impulse. Current studies confirm Vygotsky's belief that make-believe play can improve self-regulation, especially in highly impulsive children.
- *Abstract, Higher-Level Thinking*: Make-believe play also encourages abstract thinking. For example, when a child pretends to "ride" a block as if it were a horse, the child separates the idea of qualities that make up a horse from the horse and attaches them to the block—a precursor for the development of abstract thought.

2. An Example of the Social Constructivist Approach: Programs Inspired by the Schools of Reggio Emilia, Italy

Vygotsky's research has led to the development of many different social constructivist and play-based early childhood education curricula, including Tools of the Mind and the HighScope Perry Model. But the best examples of Vygotsky's social constructivist principles at work are to be found in early childhood programs inspired by the Reggio Emilia experience.

The Reggio Emilia experience with early childhood education has become the gold standard and has been deemed to be the best in the world. The "Reggio Emilia experience" is named after the city in which it originated and for the community of people who were dedicated to changing the culture of early childhood.

After World War II had seriously damaged their city, the community of Reggio Emilia came together and decided that the rebuilding process must be focused upon children and their early education. In a city torn by violence, the leaders were determined to place children at the center of policymaking. They dedicated themselves to establishing a new kind of education in which children are vital, contributing members of the democratic community and in which the community is an active participant in the development and well-being of children and their families.

Loris Malaguzzi, pioneering Italian teacher and psychologist, played a leading role in articulating and realizing these goals. With Malaguzzi's assistance, the city of Reggio Emilia created and officially opened the city's first municipal preschool in 1963 and played a leadership role in the establishment of Italy's national system of early childhood services.

The educators in Reggio Emilia were guided by the fundamental image of the child as a capable, caring, creative, curious, and connected member of the community. Their schools were designed to realize the goal of all parents that their children be taken seriously, be believed in, and be encouraged to reach their rich and overlooked potential.

The Reggio Emilia early childhood centers originally envisioned by Malaguzzi now have greatly expanded with municipal support and public funding. The Reggio Emilia experience has become a model for national and international campaigns for public early childhood programs for all children. Education experts throughout the world have visited Reggio Emilia's learning centers, and Reggio-inspired practices are now being used in outstanding early childhood education programs in the United States.

While it is difficult to capture the richness and depth of the teacher-child interactions that comprise the Reggio Emilia experience, the following pillars are central to it:

- A critical importance of the "image of the child" that recognizes the child's creative, intellectual, and communicative abilities and potential
- An interpretation of schools as systems of relations—the well-being of children is interdependent with the well-being of teachers and families
- The value of doubt and uncertainty as ethical premises and incentives for teachers to dedicate themselves to learning

Based upon these pillars, educators in Reggio Emilia have created early learning centers in which: (1) the environment is a "teacher" that encourages the co-construction of knowledge through relationships; (2) the curriculum emerges from and inspires children's curiosities, relies on teachers' collaborative research, and values multiple forms of representation; and (3) the learning of each child and the community is made visible through documentation.

a. An Environment That Teaches

The Reggio Emilia experience supports the creation by professional and deeply valued educators of a learning environment that facilitates a child's co-construction of his or her own cognitive, social, and emotional powers through meaningful relationships with peers, teachers, and surroundings. Reggio Emilia's schools are purposefully designed to reflect and promote the values of the community. Accordingly, the environment includes a large central space, natural lighting, and nonindustrial furnishing and plants. The phrase *space is our third teacher* is represented in the active use of school spaces to convey both "messages and possibilities."

Materials for children's work and play (blocks, crayons, paint, paper, dishes, dolls, tools, raw materials, etc.) are within easy reach and purposefully and sometimes creatively arranged or stored to convey the message that they are important. There are spaces for large and small group activities, play, and the display of child work that are carefully designed to promote child engagement. There is a frequent use of mirrors and other reflective surfaces in open spaces, classrooms, and bathrooms. There are light boxes and light tables used to display artifacts and manipulations of objects with various degrees of translucency, demonstrating Reggio Emilia's appreciation for physics and light.

Whenever possible, large windows allow shadows and light to enter classrooms and encourage observations of the outside world. Dress-up clothes and other interesting materials for play are centrally located to invite children from different classes to play together. Kitchens are highly visible places that are frequented by both children and parents. Teachers have spaces to gather, work, and talk together. Adult-size furniture is placed in the central space and in classrooms to support adult relations.

One of the most important messages conveyed by the environment is the value of the experiences children share in the classroom. Teachers are trusted to construct the classroom space to encourage and guide children's exploration, to promote collaboration, and to allow them to express themselves in many ways. The classroom environment promotes learning processes in which children are engaging with each other and with objects of interest, exploring, constructing and representing their understandings. Photographs and examples of collaborative children's work are intentionally displayed.

In Reggio Emilia–inspired programs, spaces are designed with concrete pedagogical aims. In addition to the classroom, the children's environment also includes the school building, school grounds, neighborhood, and the city. All of these areas provide children opportunities to explore and learn.

A Reggio-inspired environment also includes attractive materials. These materials include natural, beautiful, and repurposed objects for children's expression. Natural items might include leaves, seeds, sticks, shells, and stones. Beautiful man-made objects ripe for expression might include ribbon and lace, buttons and foils, wire, and other metal objects. Repurposed materials might include safe industrial by-products and small pieces of plastic. In the hands of a child with an idea, an otherwise familiar plastic piece can represent something extraordinary.

As Cathy Topal and Lella Gandini illustrate in their influential book *Beautiful Stuff*, engaging children in the collection and sorting process inspires the children to use these materials to express their evermore complex ideas, often in three dimensions. As Lisa Daly and Miriam Beloglovsky point out in *Loose Parts: Inspiring Play in Young Children*, collections of seemingly random pieces of materials foster creativity and innovation, skills critical to becoming a contributing member of society. The teacher and the children engage together with those materials around questions or provocations that arise through dialogue. The classroom environment is designed to encourage children to engage in activities that allow them to pursue play individually or in small groups.

To promote guided play, the classroom is structured with small-group learning areas filled with interesting objects and materials (blocks, reading materials, water or sand tables), have collaborative work surfaces, have easily accessible and sorted materials for creating representations, display and store children's work, have an inviting atmosphere, and, when possible, have a thoughtful use of light. The learning areas are positioned close to other learning areas to encourage children to join resources (combining a dress-up area and a book area, or writing table).

Classrooms also display children's work, their interests, thoughts, photographs, and panels of themselves and their families to create an identity and history of the classroom. The walls are usually neutral in color to allow children's work to stand out. Mass-produced teaching charts and supplies are discouraged in place of authentic work product. Children's cubbies or personal spaces should reflect what is meaningful to them, including objects or photos of family and friends and their own creations. Their photos adorn their personal mailboxes and nap spaces, and full-length mirrors are placed around the room to allow children to see their whole bodies from multiple perspectives while working.

The classroom also includes furniture that invites children to collaborate, engage, and discover their own capabilities. Ladders show children they are able to climb, adult-sized furniture and real utensils give children the opportunity to stretch their behaviors, and breakable glassware illustrates to all that young children can use and respect beautiful and fragile objects. All of these materials are accessible to the children in reachable spaces and transparent storage units. The children also have access to a variety of work surfaces, including tables of different heights. The environment includes mobile furniture and materials to facilitate learning relationships of various sizes, and to enable children to observe themselves and their world from multiple perspectives.

The learning environment does not stop at the classroom walls. Where possible, common indoor and outdoor space is a vital part of the learning community. Entryways to the classrooms are designed to connect the school to the community and the classrooms to one another. Classroom doorways are often open, welcoming, engaging, and informative. These areas display children's work and portfolios of children's explorations over time. Parents and caregivers are invited in and made to feel welcome to speak with the teacher, view their children's work, and become active partners in the learning community. The learning environment also encompasses areas outside the school building, where children are encouraged to explore with all of their senses. Rain, puddles, dew, mud, flora, and fauna often capture the interest of children.

b. An Emergent and Negotiated Curriculum

Within a fully engaged environment, a Reggio-inspired early learning center also reflects: (1) a negotiated curriculum that emerges from dialogue among professional educators, children, and their families; (2) projects that arise naturally from the interests of groups of children and that are as short or long as seem constructive; (3) the representation and presentation of concepts in multiple forms of expression, materials, and media, including spoken and written language, print, art, construction, music, puppetry, play, and drama; and (4) collaboration among children, among teachers, and among children and teachers, including dialogue, negotiation, problem solving, listening, and respect for different perspectives.

Loris Malaguzzi believed that a child has "one hundred languages . . . one hundred ways of thinking of playing, of speaking . . . and a hundred hundred hundred more." A Reggio-inspired classroom does not deprive the child of these languages; rather, it encourages children to represent their understanding in multiple ways.

Malaguzzi also recognized the intimate relationship between creativity and intelligence and hired an atelierista, or art educator, to work closely with teachers and with children. Creative expression cannot be separated from thinking. Educators ask children to communicate their knowledge through observational drawings and sculptures.

Art is not construed as an activity separate and apart from disciplines such as mathematics, science, and literacy. In fact, Reggio-inspired educators understand that learning for children includes aspects of all disciplines. Forms of expression that are traditionally categorized as "art" are a vital and integrated aspect of thinking, exploration, and communication in Reggio Emilia classrooms.

Children have daily opportunities to experiment with a variety of materials and tools, including clay, paint, sculpture, and pen and pencil to represent and share their understandings. Children are often challenged to revisit, revise, and reshape their own representations of their thinking. Children's work serves as a valuable tool for the co construction of new understandings with peers and adults.

Curriculum goals in Reggio Emilia are defined in terms of broadly construed cultural values such as developing relationships or learning how to collaborate. Long-term projects emerge from questions posed by children. The children share the project with their peers, teachers, families, and the surrounding community. Teachers, working together, also use what they learn about children's interests and understandings in the course of explorations to design challenging additional project work that promotes the development of new skills and understandings. In a Reggio-inspired early childhood learning environment, children are not only respected, they are given some control over their own learning. Donna Davilla and Susan Koenig give an example of how this occurred in one school in Reggio:

A child constructed a water wheel. The young boy had attached the water paddles at the wrong angle, and became frustrated with his work. The teacher, rather than telling him he had put them on incorrectly and giving him direct instruction, took him to the sink and allowed the water to run down the palm of his hand. She asked him to cup his hand to catch the water. Aha! He now understood why his paddles were not working. She facilitated the leap to his next level of understanding.

Similarly, in Reggio schools, educators celebrate the diversity in backgrounds and perspectives that children and families bring to the learning environment. The city of Reggio Emilia has become increasingly diverse in the past decade. The educators in Reggio Emilia understand the integration of immigrant families into the centers and schools as an opportunity for tremendous growth and learning.

Moreover, children with special needs, or "special rights" as they are called in Reggio Emilia, are not limited by adult perceptions of their cognitive functioning and are included in all activities. Children with special rights are not defined by perceived limitations. Rather, they are fully included in a classroom in Reggio Emilia, and are respected for their capability to use all their senses to learn through play, touching, dancing, moving, listening, seeing, and creating.

Educators in Reggio welcome parents and guardians as partners in designing and implementing the negotiated curriculum. Regular meetings are scheduled to encourage all to come together. The school becomes the hub of the community, fostering developmentally appropriate learning for children and adults.

c. Making Learning Visible through Documentation

The Reggio Emilia experience also reflects the work of highly skilled educators who research and learn along with students while listening, observing, and documenting the growth of community in the classroom. These teachers provide authentic assessment through documentation of a variety of learning experiences, which is then used as a tool for additional learning and advocacy for children.

Documentation is the practice of observing, recording, interpreting, and sharing through a variety of media the process and products of individual and community learning. It makes visible to multiple stakeholders the learning that takes place in an early childhood education program. Documentation is central to teachers' roles as researchers in the classrooms. Teachers take photographs, collect artifacts, and record the children's conversations. They then reflect on this data—sometimes with other teachers and frequently with the children's parents and family members—to make sense of what has been learned and to plan next steps.

The art educator, or atelierista, is also a part of the process and records the children's activities. Documentation enables all members of the learning community to construct and to share their knowledge. Documentation efforts are used as a professional development tool and are also used to make learning visible in shared spaces.

In Reggio Emilia, documentation is a means of keeping parents involved in and informed about their children's experiences, and inviting them to participate in the process. Images of families and artifacts from the families' homes are shared in the classroom. Parents are informed about and contribute to curricular decisions because of documentation and meetings focused on ongoing events in the classroom. Where appropriate, meetings with the wider school community also are documented and shared.

Vital to the development of a Reggio-inspired social constructivist learning environment are relationships between teachers, children, families, and the community. Documentation is a critical part of creating these connections.

d. Democratic Pillars

The fundamental belief that children construct their knowledge through meaningful relationships creates a foundation from which children are inspired to become engaged citizens. If a community's schools recognize and develop in children their capacity to be active participants in the construction of their own knowledge, those schools also will prepare children to become active and empowered participants in a truly democratic regime.

Accordingly, the Reggio Emilia experience is built upon a strong social constructivist foundation and the following "democratic" pillars:

D ocumentation: Teachers actively listen and observe children's learning in order to make learning visible to multiple stakeholders and to decipher children's interests, feelings, and ideas. To create such records, teachers take notes, photos, or videotape children's learning. This documentation can be shared with other teachers, children, and parents, and can also be displayed as formal public communications in the form of books, blogs, or slideshows.

E mergent Negotiated Curriculum: What has been described in the United States as emergent negotiated curriculum is an extended learning process, given shape by educators, that is driven by children's interests and discoveries as they tackle a particular question posed by a child or an adult. It requires teachers and children to listen, observe, reflect, negotiate, and respond to one another in real time. As teachers scaffold the learning process, they observe and document what the children are pursuing and representing, and guide children according to certain learning objectives. Teachers do not set a predetermined outcome. Rather, the learning process changes based on children's discoveries and questions that follow. Teachers take the child's perspective, while relying for direction on their own reflection and documentation of student learning.

This way of teaching and learning by teachers with children cycles through several steps, not necessarily in a linear fashion: listening, observing, documenting, interpreting, projecting, deciding, planning, hypothesizing, scaffolding, and back to listening and observing. The first part of the emergent curriculum requires teachers to observe and document children's actions, interactions, and representations through various media. Teachers then reflect upon and interpret the interests being expressed by the child or children. Teachers next interpret and confirm that interest with the children, and provide opportunities for children to participate, often in small groups, in collaborative related activities.

Throughout the activities, teachers and children interact and co-construct understandings. During this time, teachers continue to observe and document the children's behavior and engagement, and take note of any newly expressed interest or ideas. Teachers then use any newly formed or expressed interests to create different, additional activities.

While in this process, teachers also develop in children the ability to experience themselves as active, self-directed agents who can, individually and in collaboration with others, formulate personally meaningful learning goals, figure out strategies to achieve them, engage the world to pursue them, construct understandings, and communicate the newly developed understandings to others. Children strengthen their capacity to make connections, to communicate, to observe, to reason, to represent their ideas in various media, and to share these ideas with peers and adults.

M ultiple Perspectives: Reggio-inspired teachers encourage children to consider multiple points of view when pondering a question or object of inquiry in order to expand the children's range or depth of their understanding. Children can then compare their viewpoints and learn that their own views may differ from those of their peers. This dialogue is important for children to engage in, as it is crucial for children, like adults, to connect with other children and to become more aware of others' perspectives.

O ne-Hundred Languages: Reggio-inspired educators are inspired in their practice with children by the insight in Loris Malaguzzi's poem titled "No Way. The Hundred Is There." They believe it is their responsibility to provide opportunities for children to express their ideas in countless ways. The poem's metaphor of "one hundred languages" also leads educators to reject arbitrary separation of head and hands, listening and speaking, science and imagination, and work and play. In its place, these educators embrace the whole child and recognize that children are always constructing knowledge across traditional disciplines.

C ollaboration: The educational environment is infused with collaborations between children, between children and teachers, between teachers and families, and between the school and the community. Small groups provide opportunity for meaningful interactions and shared discovery. Moreover, teachers model collaboration by sharing with each other their research about learning. After documenting their observations, for example, teachers reflect with one another on their findings, plan extensions of children's learning, hypothesize possible outcomes, and collaborate to implement activities and different ways to structure their classrooms.

R esearchers: Children are natural "researchers" as they question what they see, predict outcomes, experiment, and dissect their discoveries. When children participate in long-term learning projects, they have an opportunity to continue to become a "researcher" as they learn, explore, and look closely at their understanding of the world around them. As highly respected researchers, teachers also approach their work with children with inquisitive minds, rather than with preset assumptions and goals.

A telier: Reggio-inspired schools have or aspire to have an atelier, or at least some common space for students to work on projects involving several different mediums, such as clay, wire, mirrors, paper, paints, and other objects. When not possible, mini-ateliers in classrooms or mobile studios are developed. Ideally, each school would also have an atelierista, or studio educator with a strong background in visual arts. The studio educator supports the children and teachers by finding commonalities in children's interests across classrooms, by providing an artist's knowledge of a wide range of materials, and by offering a shared space for expression.

T ime to Explore: Teachers have sufficient time to follow the curiosities of children inspired to pursue long-term projects or in-depth studies of a question or provocation. Children engaged in projects have an opportunity to become disciplined researchers, they observe, hypothesize solutions, reflect on their findings, and reanalyze their original hypotheses.

I mage of the Child: Reggio Emilia educators understand that children are capable, creative, curious, caring, and connected members of their community who have tremendous strengths and capabilities. The most recent evidence from cognitive neuroscience and developmental psychology confirms this image of the child. With that proper image, teachers aim to challenge children's thinking, empower children to be curious, and facilitate children's ability to connect with the world and create understandings. As a teacher continues to view children as strong, deep, and powerful, the children will become this image, and become active questioners who construct knowledge and meaning.

C ommunity: This genuinely democratic early childhood education requires a professional educator who partners with families and the community. Teachers view parents or guardians as fully engaged participants in their children's education. Teachers engage in a regular meetings with parents, teachers, and other staff members for everyone to share perspectives, learn, and deepen their understanding of this learning approach. The meetings often include whole-group dialogues that relate to some portion of child development. During this time, shared documentation of children's learning, such as a drawn representation of an object in nature, enables many to reflect on children's deep thinking. This type of community discussion exposes parents to others' perspectives and provides a forum to discuss the goals of education.

Teachers create a classroom environment that is welcoming to parents and encourages them to engage with teachers. Family members are invited into the classroom to share experiences and cultural practices. Once a relationship is developed between a teacher and parent, teachers can more easily make visible to the parent the child's interests and growth. Parents, in turn, after learning of new interests, are then able to engage their children at home around these interests.

Teachers share children's learning and exploration with parents through portfolios that document children's pleasure of learning and growth. They are kept in the classroom of the children with each child's name, visible to children and to families. They will be kept in the school until the end of the time the children are in the learning center, and then the children themselves will hand them to their families the last day at the center to celebrate their work and to take them home.

Portfolios are designed to share the strengths and interests of a child operating as a member of a learning community. Teachers also engage family members by asking them to enter in the classroom every day—for a few minutes if possible—when they accompany them. In Italy, grandparents may play that role, as Italian extended families tend to live close and help young working parents. Parents also form an organization and elect representatives among them that are in dialogue with the city school administration.

All of these interactions allow teachers to understand parents' feelings and ideas while also allowing parents to value the abilities of their child. Parents and teachers "co-construct" understandings about children. Lastly, these parent-teacher interactions provide teachers with opportunities to share their perspectives of teaching and learning with parents. Parents then are better able to incorporate what they learn from teachers and the educational process into their relationship with their children.

In a Reggio-inspired early childhood education program, the community beyond the doors of the school is a vital partner in the learning. The community provides a forum for children's expression in common spaces. The city or town surrounding the school may become involved in a community-wide activity. For example, if children begin to explore their questions about bicycles and how they work, the community may decide to explore those same questions. The children's representations drawn during their studies may be displayed for adult reflection in a shared space (e.g., on walls of a railroad underpass). Or, where children and teachers explore questions about lines in leaves, the surrounding city may explore questions about lines of transportation or lines of authority.

Not only do children learn outside of their school walls but also community members learn to appreciate the abilities of young children to construct knowledge. Through documentation, Reggio-inspired educators make visible to the community surrounding the school the learning that takes place within. This form of authentic assessment provides to community stakeholders, including policymakers, taxpayers, and funding sources, evidence of the profound effectiveness of the children's experience.

Children emerge from a Reggio-inspired early childhood experience with the executive functioning skills that they need to lead, to create, to problem solve, to collaborate, to express themselves, to negotiate, to build alliances, to focus, to listen, to absorb, to relate to adults, and to find joy in learning. They also develop a deeply rooted sense of self-confidence and an authentic sense of self-respect and self-esteem. By creating a community of early learning environments in which children are encouraged to construct their own knowledge through meaningful relationships, the educators in Reggio Emilia have developed an exemplary experience founded upon social constructivist premises and democratic pillars.

Chapter Four

Why Should I Strongly Consider Choosing a Program That Follows the Social Constructivist Approach to Early Childhood Education?

Tell me and I forget, teach me and I may remember, involve me and I learn.
—Benjamin Franklin

A. THE SOCIAL CONSTRUCTIVIST APPROACH PRODUCES EDUCATIONAL, SOCIAL, AND ECONOMIC BENEFITS FOR ALL CHILDREN

There is now an impressive body of data comparing the efficacy of various approaches to early childhood education. The results are in. The evidence is clear that the most effective early childhood education programs use social constructivist practices by which teachers encourage children to develop their capacity to construct knowledge by building meaningful relationships with their families, caregivers, teachers, peers, and surrounding communities.

These social constructivist practices teach children the vital habits of mind and heart that they will need for their future success and well-being. Howard Gardner—one of the nation's most influential educational psychologists—concludes that education must be directed toward creating habits of mind that will be valuable in the future, not the past. He shows that in the future, individuals who wish to thrive must develop five different kinds of "minds" or "capacities":

- A disciplined mind—the ability to become an expert in at least one area
- A synthesizing mind—the ability to gather information from many sources, to organize the information in helpful ways and to communicate the information to others
- A creating mind—the ability of adults to keep alive in themselves the mind and sensibility of a young child, including an insatiable curiosity about other people and the environment, an openness to untested paths, a willingness to struggle, and a desire and capacity to learn from failure
- A respectful mind—the ability to understand the perspectives and motivations of others, particularly those who appear to be different
- An ethical mind—the ability to appreciate one's social or professional role and to act in accordance with shared standards for that role

Early childhood programs that develop the ability to engage in meaningful relationships are far more likely to develop these critical habits of mind and heart than are the programs that concentrate primarily on what many think of as traditional academic achievement.

The longitudinal study of children enrolled in the HighScope Perry Preschool program in Ypsilanti, Michigan, helps us to understand why a school's philosophy of education matters. Children were divided into two groups—one that did not receive any formal education program, and one that was given a high-quality early childhood education program. The children in the treatment group who were given a high-quality early childhood education program were then subdivided into three groups. Each group was given a different early childhood education delivery model:

- The "Direct Instruction" model, in which teachers initiated drill and practice activities designed to reward children for responding correctly to a predetermined set of tests to measure academic performance
- The "Nursery School" model, in which teachers facilitated self-initiated play for students and introduced projects in a relatively unstructured, supportive environment
- The "HighScope" Perry model, in which teachers arranged the classroom and daily routine to enable active learning by children, who play and engage in their own activities in small and large groups and who are observed to determine whether they demonstrate key developmental indicators

All aspects of the treatment group's early childhood education programs were identical, except for the delivery model. After one year of pre-K, the overall average IQ of children in all three groups rose 27 points, from a borderline level of 78 to a normal range level of 105.

Some critics of investing in early childhood programs like to point out that the average IQ of these children dissipated over time and settled at 95, within the normal range. These critics also point to a few other studies suggesting that any gains from early childhood education programs fade out when children reach third grade. But these critics miss the point. The benefits of early childhood education programs cannot be measured in a snapshot standardized test in third grade.

Rather, the positive impact of the Perry project and social constructivist programs must be assessed based on lifelong outcomes. By age twenty-three, the differences in those outcomes for the three Perry early childhood education approaches were remarkable. Children who received the Nursery School and HighScope models showed tremendous advantages over those children who received the Direct Instruction program.

In fact, the HighScope group had eight significant advantages over the Direct Instruction group, including fewer felony arrests, fewer arrests for property crimes, fewer years requiring treatment for emotional impairment or disturbance, fewer anger management issues, less teen misconduct, a higher percentage living with spouse, more who planned to graduate from college, and more who did volunteer work.

The HighScope model is designed to implement the social-constructivist principles of Lev Vygotsky, by which children are encouraged to engage with adults, peers, and their environment to construct their own knowledge. The HighScope curriculum stressed collaboration, the development of meaningful interpersonal relations, and interpersonal skills.

Based upon his sophisticated analysis of all of the available data regarding early childhood education programs, Nobel Prize–winning economist James Heckman concludes:

> Success in life depends on personality traits that are not well captured by measures of cognition. Conscientiousness, perseverance, sociability and curiosity matter.

The ability to engage in meaningful relationships, and to use executive function to facilitate focus and perseverance, leads directly to positive educational achievement, labor market performance, and health.

Heckman notes that relationship-building skills promote learning, even as measured in achievement test scores. A child's achievement test scores are directly attributable to these social skills. Children who perform poorly on traditional standardized tests nonetheless do well in life if early interventions have developed those skills. On the other hand, children who perform well on traditional standardized tests nonetheless do poorly in life if they have not developed such relationship-building skills.

Accordingly, the social constructivist approach to early childhood education produces significantly greater long-term benefits than the direct-instruction approach. Children in social constructivist early childhood education environments far surpass those in direct instruction environments in skills critical to success in life, particularly collaboration, executive function, and perseverance. Moreover, children educated in social constructivist environments actually surpass their direct instruction peers on academic achievement tests measured over time.

In the hands of a skilled educator, direct instruction may be used effectively within a social-constructivist environment to help inform the choices that children can make. Yet the evidence shows that the long-term educational, economic, and social benefits of a social constructivist *approach* to early childhood education significantly surpass those from a tightly structured direct instruction approach.

Despite this overwhelming evidence, families still may be tempted to push for programs that prioritize the direct instruction of traditional academic skills. Their temptation may be based on their assumption that children who do not acquire traditionally defined math and literacy skills at home "need" the direct instruction of those skills at school and are not "ready" for social constructivist approaches to education. Parents also may assume that social constructivist practices are more expensive than direct instruction. Both assumptions, however, are unfounded.

As the numerous studies and data sets show, the social constructivist approach has been proven to achieve remarkable results for all children, regardless of their race, ethnicity, or socioeconomic status. Moreover, although highly trained and valued teachers are indispensable to any effective early childhood education program, social constructivist practices need not be any more expensive than other early learning approaches. The benefits of attracting, educating, and appropriately compensating teachers who engage in social constructivist practices far exceed the costs.

In fact, in order to test the impact of the Reggio Emilia approach on children's learning outcomes, researchers specifically examined data from seventy-four Reggio-inspired programs. These programs are located in racially and economically diverse communities from across the United States. Many of them are connected with Head Start, or are otherwise available for a relatively modest fee.

The results of the existing data are clear and compelling: the social constructivist approach, exemplified by the Reggio Emilia experience, is effective in supporting the learning of all children. This is true in public early childhood education programs, private programs, public-private partnerships, and Head Start classrooms.

B. RECENT DISCOVERIES IN BRAIN RESEARCH DEMONSTRATE HOW THE SOCIAL CONSTRUCTIVIST APPROACH HELPS CHILDREN

The most recent neuroscience research reveals precisely how and why an investment of resources in social constructivist early childhood education programs has produced benefits, and will continue to produce remarkable educational, social, and economic benefits. Relying on sophisticated research techniques including brain imaging, the world's foremost neuroscientists and cognitive psychologists have discovered that a child's brain is transformed by meaningful relationships in the child's early learning environment. Children are naturally capable, curious, caring, and empathetic. They are hardwired to pursue meaningful relationships, which are critical to the development of their mental processes.

These relationships can first be seen in the wondrous nonverbal communication that occurs when a primary caretaker responds reflectively to an infant's crying, cooing, mimicking, laughing, smiling, and gesturing. Young children who learn to build or to rebuild these meaningful relationships in early learning environments achieve remarkable lifelong success and well-being. These profound relationships develop in social constructivist early childhood education programs when children join with their classmates and teachers to explore the materials in their environment and to share their reflections on their evolving understanding of their place in the community.

These early learning environments help to build a child's natural desire and capacity for:

- Attachment (the ability to form and maintain emotionally significant, reliable, and enduring bonds with others)
- Intersubjectivity (the ability to perceive, respect, and respond to the thoughts, feelings, and intentions of others)
- Cognitive integration (the ability to marshal associations, intuitions, calculations, and memories)
- Well-being (physical and mental health)
- Executive function (the ability to control impulses, to maintain focus, and to make and implement flexible plans)

These relationship-building capacities are sometimes belittled as "soft" skills that must be distinguished from hard academic skills such as literacy and math. But there is nothing soft about them. Neuroscientists have now demonstrated that these capacities are inextricably tied to cognition itself. They are critical to a child's development of indispensable habits of mind such as discipline, synthesis, creativity, respect, and ethics. It is these particular habits of mind—rather than just traditionally tested academic skills—that significantly increase the chances that a child will grow to experience life-long success and well-being, regardless of the child's race, ethnicity, or socioeconomic status.

1. The Social Constructivist Approach Develops Healthy Attachment Relationships

Cognitive abilities are intertwined with all other human motivation, including attachment. Meaningful attachment relationships based on genuine communication support the development of social, emotional, and cognitive functioning.

Early attachment experiences alter the chemicals in the brain that develop the nervous system's capacity to support emotional resilience. Social interactions and attachments that are perceived to be positive support emotional resilience, while those that are negative diminish emotional resilience in children and may make it more difficult for them to adjust to stressful events in the future. The lack of a healthy primary attachment relationship can have a detrimental effect on a child's ability to build relationships with others. Security of attachment, on the other hand, allows a child to develop a healthy sense of self and resilience—the ability to overcome the effects of negative consequences or experiences.

Children who experience reciprocal responsiveness in early learning environments associated with a secure attachment also are more likely to exhibit focus, perseverance, and control over their behavior. The security in feeling that a disruption in the relationship will be repaired allows a child to develop grit and resiliency in the face of life's inevitable hardships. By building or rebuilding a child's capacity for attachment, a social constructivist learning environment therefore develops the child's socio-emotional control and perseverance in the face of negative events and challenges.

The forms of attachment that are supported in a social constructivist learning environment develop in children habits of mind and heart that are vital to their lifelong success and well-being:

First, meaningful attachment relationships in an early learning environment enable children to develop habits of sharing and amplifying positive emotional states (such as joy and elation) and sharing and comforting negative states (such as fear and sadness).

Second, meaningful relationships enable children to develop habits of collaboration, empathy, and emotional communication.

Third, meaningful relationships enable children to develop habits of contingent communication in which the verbal and nonverbal signals of a peer or educator are precisely responsive to the child's. The mind of the child is joined with another person at a basic level of emotion, and each person "feels felt" by the other.

Fourth, meaningful relationships enable children to develop habits of reflective dialogue. Each participant feels comfortable sharing and does share their own mental processes, including thoughts, emotions, memories, beliefs, and ideas.

Fifth, meaningful relationships enable children to develop habits of reestablishing relationships when they inevitably become interrupted or disrupted.

Sixth, meaningful relationships enable children to develop habits of joining together with others to co-construct their knowledge about the world by sharing coherent stories about the past, present, and future.

Seventh, meaningful relationships enable children to develop the habits of perseverance and self-regulation when confronted with challenging experiences and emotions. In a meaningful relationship, the emotional connection survives pain and difficult feelings. It is enduring and reliable.

Eighth, meaningful relationships enable children to develop habits of providing and receiving emotional warmth steadfastly and predictably provided over an extended period of time.

Finally, a relationship built upon reflective communication enables children to assess their own process of constructing knowledge, which helps them to refine those particular learning strategies that are successful for them.

2. The Social Constructivist Approach Develops Intersubjectivity

Intersubjectivity is the process by which young children develop the capacity to understand the thoughts, feelings, and intentions of others. It is the foundation for empathy, which is critical to human survival, learning, and well-being.

Early childhood education environments that use a social constructivist approach provide this opportunity for children. In exercising their natural disposition toward intersubjectivity, individuals find great joy; they realize what they have in common with others.

Children are motivated to cooperate and have the capacity to engage in altruism and cooperation. They are also able to exchange roles with others. Intersubjectivity thus has what John Barresi and Chris Moore refer to as a "ubiquitous role that permeates all other mental functions and makes us uniquely human." By building a child's capacity for intersubjectivity, a social constructivist learning program enables the child to recognize, respect, and respond to the thoughts, feelings, and intentions of others.

3. The Social Constructivist Approach Develops the Healthy Integration of Cognitive Processes

As Dr. Daniel J. Siegel has found: "We come into the world wired to make connections with one another, and the subsequent neural shaping of our brain, the very foundation of our sense of self, is built upon these intimate exchanges between the infant and the caregiver. In the early years, this interpersonal regulation is essential for survival, but throughout our lives we continue to need such connections for a sense of vitality and well-being."

According to Siegel, healthy early childhood relationships transform the prefrontal cortex in the brain, thereby integrating the cognitive processes that are essential to success and well-being, including: (1) bodily regulation; (2) attuned communication; (3) emotional balance; (4) response flexibility; (5) fear modulation; (6) empathy; (7) insight; (8) moral awareness; and (9) intuition.

The meaningful relationships supported in a social constructivist early learning environment develop this healthy "integration." Siegel demonstrates that well-being and higher-order mental processing skills require an integrated mind, one in which apparently disparate components of mental processes such as thoughts and feelings, logic and intuition are linked to each other through extremely active synaptic connections. These connections are vital to coherent cognitive functioning, empathy, self-regulation, resilience, health, and well-being.

Social constructivist early childhood education programs are designed to support these connections. By strengthening a child's ability to develop meaningful relationships, social constructivist early childhood education programs necessarily also strengthen a child's cognition.

Such relationships also can be developed between individuals when they experience materials in their environment. David Hawkins writes brilliantly about the relationship that forms between a child, a teacher, and such materials. The relationship is formed from respect. He notes that, when a teacher explores an object with a child, the teacher has made possible a "relation between the child and 'It.'" The material is a foundation for communicating with the teacher on a new level.

He recognizes that the relationships that a child forms with teachers, peers, and materials allow the child to develop the indispensable "capacity for synthesis, for building a stable framework within which many episodes of experience can be put together coherently." The child's ability to explore new relationships, to differentiate those relationships, and to integrate them into the child's evolving sense of reality of the world is vital to that child's well-being. By supporting the development in children of the capacity to build meaningful relationships, social constructivist programs facilitate the healthy integration of mental processes that is indispensable to learning.

4. The Social Constructivist Approach Develops Habits of Well-Being

The single most important factor in fostering happiness and well-being is the quality of a person's relationships. Children who have developed the ability to form and maintain meaningful relationships are happy and healthy adults. They are significantly happier and healthier than their peers who do not have such meaningful relationships. Moreover, those children who have formed meaningful relationships are even happier and healthier than their wealthier peers who have not formed those relationships.

In "A Survey Method for Characterizing Daily Experience: The Day Reconstruction Method," Daniel Kahneman and his colleagues present their transformative research regarding the determinants of happiness and well-being. The evidence indicates that individuals experience the greatest degree of happiness from their social relationships.

Significantly, income has far less impact on happiness than relationships. Although extremely low levels of household income can create stresses of subsistence that greatly diminish happiness, levels of wealth above subsistence have no statistically significant connection to happiness.

Every reliable study conducted after Professor Kahneman presented his research has confirmed that the most significant determinant of happiness—whether measured as momentary feelings, reflective thoughts, or life satisfaction—is the quality of a person's relationships. In fact, he finds that the evidence shows that "very happy people" differ from unhappy or modestly happy people in the level of their "fulsome and satisfying interpersonal lives."

The quality of relationships also is connected to physical well-being, health, and wellness. Meaningful relationships increase immunity to disease and infection, lower the risk of heart disease, and reduce the degree of cognitive decline through the aging process. Indeed, the absence of meaningful relationships is as deleterious to health as obesity or smoking. It is not surprising, therefore, that James Heckman, in *Giving Kids a Fair Chance (A Strategy That Works)*, presents irrefutable evidence that early childhood programs that develop in children the capacity to build meaningful relationships actually produce significant health advantages, including a reduction in obesity, blood pressure, and hypertension.

5. The Social Constructivist Approach Develops Executive Function

The concept of executive function is a hot topic these days. You may have heard recent conversations about the importance of "grit" or "mindset" to early learning. These popular catch phrases capture some, but not all, of the power of executive function.

Executive function properly understood includes three types of capacities: working memory, cognitive flexibility, and inhibitory control. These capacities enable individuals to make plans, stay focused, and control impulses.

Working memory is the ability to collect and manage information in the mind for short periods of time so that the information can be immediately used. Cognitive flexibility is the ability to adjust mental strategies to meet changing circumstances, including the ability to try different approaches to solving problems, resolving conflict, and overcoming obstacles. Inhibitory control is the capacity to master impulses, resist temptations, and avoid distractions. In its absence, people act entirely upon their immediate feelings, lose focus and attention, and pursue instant gratification.

As author Paul Tough has observed, and as the latest economic and brain research confirms, executive function provides an important link between early school achievement and social, emotional, and moral development. The National Scientific Council on the Developing Child and the National Forum on Early Childhood Policy and Programs state in their working paper that children who do not develop their executive function in early childhood "have a very hard time managing the routine tasks of daily life." Their working paper concludes: "Children with stronger working memory, inhibitors and attentional skills also have been found to make larger gains on tests of early math, language, literacy development during the preschool years than their peers with weaker executive function skills."

Executive function is particularly predictive of future academic success in math and reading among children from "economically disadvantaged" families. Children who do not grow executive function skills not only have difficulty in school, they also display significantly more confrontational and antisocial behaviors as adults. A child whose brain has developed executive function in early learning environments is better able to manage stress throughout life.

Although children have an innate genetic predisposition toward executive function, they do not simply acquire executive function through the mere passage of time. Children do not just "outgrow" their inabilities to focus, control impulses, or adjust to challenging circumstances. Their early learning experiences are crucial to the development of their executive function.

As such, children should not be blamed for their failure to acquire grit. Nor can the educational system's failure to provide adequate resources to children be excused by the mistaken suggestion that a child should simply develop grit to overcome the hardships caused by the lack of those resources. To the contrary, early childhood education programs should be made available to all children so that they may develop capacities such as grit and executive function.

There is overwhelming evidence that social constructivist programs that develop in children the capacity to build meaningful relationships thereby also develop their executive function. Children who receive an early child-hood education based on the social constructivist approach show significant improvement in executive function capacities compared with children who receive an early childhood education focused on traditional academic skills.

Early childhood education programs that enable children to develop meaningful, positive relationships are particularly effective in supporting the growth of executive function. Through cooperative relationships with peers, children necessarily exercise their executive function muscles. They must control their own impulses and emotions, they must collect and manipulate information, they must eliminate distractions and focus on a shared objective, and they must be flexible in response to any problems or obstacles they encounter. A child who learns to engage in constructive social relationships thereby also learns habits of mind that are vital to demonstrating traditional academic achievement: dedicated memory, cognitive activity, focus, and self-control.

Executive function is also promoted in an environment in which children have meaningful, positive relationships with educators. Such educators will appreciate the child's progress in developing executive capabilities and will allow children to take reasonable risks. Being allowed to struggle and fail provides young children with opportunities to persevere and build resiliency. A wise educator outfits the environment to present challenges, mental and physical, to children, while remaining present to scaffold until the child is able to perform without assistance.

A meaningful, positive relationship between the child and the educator is the foundation that allows the child to take risks that will ultimately result in the child's ability to exercise executive function independently. Where that relationship exists, the educator is attuned to the underlying reasons that a child may not have yet developed executive capabilities and will be able to support the child in strengthening those capabilities.

An educator who instead punishes the child for exhibiting an inability to exercise executive function actually exacerbates the cause of that inability. Punishment or threats of punishment increase the stress levels in the child that make control more difficult. In addition, when an educator punishes a child for displaying a symptom of inadequate attachment or integration, the educator actually frustrates the creation of a relationship with the child that might replicate, repair, or replace healthy primary attachment and integra-tion. The teacher who dismisses the child's behavior by punishing the behav-ior without being attentive to the emotional cause effectively abandons the child, reinforcing a pattern of relationships that are antithetical to learning and well-being.

Similarly, a teacher who responds to a child's struggles with executive function by requiring the child to "sit still and learn" traditional math or literacy skills is only further frustrating that child's efforts to develop executive function. A child who is still developing a working memory, cognitive flexibility, and self-control does not benefit from lesson plans likely to frustrate or inhibit the expression of those functions. Conversely, when a teacher supports a child's development of executive function by attending to the relational issues at play, the teacher also simultaneously develops the child's capacity to engage in genuine literacy and mathematics.

After reviewing all of the evidence, therefore, the Harvard Graduate School of Education concludes: "Early education policies that emphasize literacy instruction alone are missing an important opportunity to increase their effectiveness by including attention to the development of executive function skills." Early childhood education programs that are designed to develop executive function, by contrast, not only improve student performance in traditional academic subjects; they also establish an indispensable foundation for success and well-being throughout life.

Chapter Five

What Is the Best Approach to Discipline in an Early Childhood Education Program?

Do not train a child to learn by force or harshness; but direct them to it by what amuses their minds, so that you may be better able to discover with accuracy the peculiar bent of the genius of each.
—Plato

Early childhood education programs have a variety of approaches to discipline. In selecting a particular program, families should be attuned to whether the program approaches discipline in an appropriate manner.

A. CORPORAL PUNISHMENT AND PHYSICAL RESTRAINTS

Corporal punishment is discipline that deliberately inflicts pain upon a child and includes any physical punishment such as spanking. In many states, corporal punishment is unlawful. If corporal punishment is lawful in your state, you should determine whether the early childhood program that you are considering uses any form of corporal punishment in its practices. If so, parents should avoid that program like the plague. The evidence is absolutely clear. Corporal punishment or any form of physical restraint does not work. It does not correct or redirect a child's behavior, and it only harms the child. Programs that use corporal punishment not only are not up to date with current best practices but also have the capacity to harm a vulnerable population.

In 2000, the American Academy of Pediatrics officially issued a recommendation that "corporal punishment be abolished in all states by law." In a comprehensive empirical and statistical study, John Guthrow recently concluded: "Clearly, those states which have banned paddling altogether and which employ more positive disciplinary measures in the classroom achieve far greater educational success and have created far more functional societies than those states which still use the paddle. That fact is simply irrefutable." Guthrow discovered an "undesirable" relationship between "paddling and pathology," such that schools in states still allowing corporal punishment produce students with "relatively lower test scores, higher drop-out rates, higher poverty rates, and lower-quality health care."

The National Association of School Psychologists also recently reaffirmed its formal policy opposing corporal punishment in schools because "[e]vidence indicates that corporal punishment negatively affects the social, psychological and educational development of students."

As educational experts began to question the effectiveness of aggressive forms of punishment, state legislatures became increasingly convinced that corporal punishment disserved the goals of education. The majority of states (twenty-seven and the District of Columbia) now have passed statutes that specifically make corporal punishment illegal. Of the states that have not yet passed statutes criminalizing corporal punishment, Texas reports the highest number of students (73,994) struck per school year, such that 22 percent of all corporal punishment in the nation is administered in Texas. In Mississippi, however, the highest *percentage* of students receives such punishment. Data released in February 2003 reveal that 9.8 percent of the students in Mississippi, or 48,627 children, received corporal punishment in the 1999 to 2000 school year.

In those states in which corporal punishment is not illegal, the most recent available evidence indicates that African American students are struck by educators at a rate that is more than two times their makeup in the population. These students comprise 17 percent of the student population in public schools throughout the United States, and receive 39 percent of the acts of corporal punishment. White students in these same schools comprise 62 percent of all students, but receive only 53 percent of the incidents of corporal punishment. In fact, the percentage of white children who are struck by educators has declined from 65 percent in 1976 to 53 percent in 2000, while the percentage of nonwhite children who are hit has increased from 29 percent in 1976 to 39 percent in 2000.

In selecting an early childhood education program, parents and caregivers should insist that the program adopts and follows a policy that forbids any form of corporal punishment. The following is an example of such a policy:

> Corporal punishment shall not be used. Corporal punishment is defined as
> slapping, paddling, restraint, or maintenance of students in physically painful

positions. The intentional infliction of physical or emotional harm is forbidden in this educational environment.

B. TIMEOUTS AND IN-SCHOOL SUSPENSIONS

Timeouts and in-school suspensions are ineffective and counterproductive. Timeouts within the classroom or school are common. They are not, howev er, often beneficial. While a child may benefit from time away from the noise and activity of the classroom to regain composure or reflect upon behavior, this should not feel like "punishment." A teacher should be close by to give the child a sense that he or she is not alone or isolated, but merely being given the time needed to calm and collect thoughts. Timeouts, in their most extreme form—suspension and expulsion—are misused and overused. Stemming from behaviorism—the belief that learning is defined as a change in observable behavior—timeouts, suspensions, and expulsions are almost always forms of punishment imposed by a person in an effort to exert his or her power to decrease unwanted behavior.

A February 2015 report from UCLA's Civil Rights Project examined national out-of-school suspension data and found that thousands of preschoolers were suspended from school at least once during the 2011 to 2012 school year—5,000 at least once and 2,500 more than once. The data showed that black children represent about 18 percent of children enrolled in preschool programs in schools, but almost half the students were suspended more than once. Overall, the data show that black students of all ages are suspended and expelled at a rate three times higher than that of white children.

Children who are not allowed to attend pre-K programs cannot possibly benefit from them. Experts assert that, further, out-of-school punishment feeds the school-to-prison pipeline by breeding student disengagement, making a child more likely to drop out of school and more likely to enter the juvenile justice system.

Connecticut, Chicago, and the District of Columbia have banned preschool suspensions for minor offenses such as disruption and defiance, citing data and describing how this has an adverse effect on the children's development. In December 2014, the U.S. Department of Health and Human Services and the U.S. Department of Education issued a policy statement and recommendations "to assist States and their public and private local early childhood programs in preventing and severely limiting expulsions and suspensions in early learning settings." The policy statement went on to recognize that expulsions and suspensions occur regularly in pre-K settings, which is especially problematic given the adverse development, health, and education outcomes using such discipline measures produces.

While you, as a parent, might believe that excluding children with challenging behaviors from your child's classroom is beneficial, ultimately your child's community will suffer the consequences. Older children denied early opportunities to learn to form meaningful relationships with peers and adults will eventually affect your child's world.

C. RESTORATIVE JUSTICE

Restorative justice is a viable alternative to punitive approaches and has proven to be the most effective method of discipline. A restorative justice approach is one that is collaborative, relies on social justice curriculum, and progresses toward building community. Restorative justice heals rather than continues a cycle of disobedience and punishment.

States and districts are recognizing that disciplining through restorative justice is far more effective than any other method. The State of Illinois, for example, has recognized the "long-standing and well-documented negative effects of exclusionary discipline" and has thus worked to adopt best practices and develop policies that reduce the time that children lose due to such policies and to eradicate inequities in how discipline is administered.

In its Model Code of Conduct, the Transforming School Discipline Collaborative for the State of Illinois notes that developing a district or school's discipline philosophy "presents a meaningful opportunity for students, parents, guardians, families, district and school staff, school board members, and community members to engage in a collaborative process that results in a shared vision to which all stakeholders can be committed. All of these stakeholders must be involved in the development, implementation, and evaluation of your discipline policies." It also sets forth components of a discipline philosophy: a discipline creed, rights and responsibilities, and a discipline framework.

An example of a discipline creed found in the Illinois Model Code of Conduct follows:

> Discipline is any policy, procedure, or consequence used by anyone at the district or school to redirect student behavior, so that all the students involved are successfully engaged in a healthy and safe school climate and culture. Discipline should be used as an opportunity for support, learning, growth, self-awareness, and community building, instead of punishment.
>
> Our goals are to understand and address the causes of behavior, resolve conflicts, encourage students to take responsibility for changing their behavior, repair the harm done, restore the relationships in the school community, and reintegrate students into the school community.
>
> We use evidence-based, school-wide discipline policies developed, implemented, monitored, evaluated, and revised with meaningful, shared, and equal input by the school community, which includes students, parents, guardians,

families, district and school staff, school board members, and community members to create a positive and inclusive school climate for everyone.

Our district and schools are committed to applying school discipline policies and practices in a fair and equitable manner so as not to disproportionately impact students of color, students with disabilities, LGBT students, students with limited English proficiency, students with unstable family and home lives, homeless students, military-involved students, students who have been the target of bullying behavior, or other at-risk students.

With regard to rights and responsibilities, the code of conduct should identify rights and responsibilities of parents, students, and teachers. Coming up with these rights and responsibilities should be a collaborative process, and, while all stakeholders will share some, others may be more specific to each stakeholder group.

With regard to the discipline framework, schools will provide positive early and differentiated interventions for students using a multitiered system of support (supports that are schoolwide, provided to groups, or provided to individual students). Students who have fallen behind, students who are being disciplined, students who are at risk of leaving or being pushed out of school, or students who are disproportionately negatively affected by policies in a school community are supported by specific academic, behavioral, mental health, and social-emotional practices at different tiers, based on data.

As such, "restorative measures" is defined in Illinois law as:

> a continuum of school-based alternatives to exclusionary discipline, such as suspensions and expulsions, that: (i) are adapted to the particular needs of the school and community, (ii) contribute to maintaining school safety, (iii) protect the integrity of a positive and productive learning climate, (iv) teach students the personal and interpersonal skills they will need to be successful in school and society, (v) serve to build and restore relationships among students, families, schools, and communities, and (vi) reduce the likelihood of future disruption by balancing accountability with an understanding of students' behavioral health needs in order to keep students in school.

The Illinois Model Code of Conduct sets forth various support services and interventions that may include:

- Referral of those who experienced harm and caused harm to appropriate support services in the school and community, such as: counselors, psychologists, social workers, child welfare attendance personnel, or other school support service personnel for case management, counseling, and anything else that may address underlying behavior
- Notification of parents, guardians, and students in writing from all those involved

- Processes for resolution, such as mediation, restorative justice circles led by an experienced circle leader, conversations, and family groups
- Conferences, behavior contracts, instruction in anger and/or stress management, and social and emotional skill building
- Academic interventions, such as tutoring and the use of formative assessment
- Community service, including opportunities to reflect on service to the community with adult mentors
- Study teams, guidance teams, resource panel teams, or other intervention-related teams that assess the behavior and develop and implement individualized plans to address the behavior in partnership with the student and parents or guardians

The district and the schools should provide structured opportunities for students, parents, guardians, families, staff, school board members, and community members to give input, get information, help make decisions, and participate in the educational process. All of these individuals must be informed in a timely and clear manner as to how and when they can participate, and trainings should be provided on how the individuals can effectively hold each other and schools accountable. There should also be a grievance and complaint procedure and issues should be resolved with due process.

Because the goal is to "create a safe and supportive environment where all students can develop the academic, social, and emotional skills needed to become engaged citizens," challenges in student conduct should be addressed in the most constructive way possible, and out-of-school suspensions and expulsions should be used only as a last resort and for legitimate educational purposes.

Chapter Six

What Is the Best Approach to Technology in an Early Childhood Education Program?

Technology is just a tool. In terms of getting the kids working together and motivating them, the teacher is the most important.
—Bill Gates

Families should look for an early childhood education program that strikes the proper balance in the use of technology and interactive media. Some programs fill their classrooms with computers and screens to distract, calm, or placate children. Other programs may advertise that they have computers and screens to ensure that young children are taught keyboarding and coding skills. They view screen time as a selling point.

But the research indicates that these uses of technology actually can be harmful to your child's development. The best early childhood programs recognize that technology is merely a material that children may choose to use to help them to establish meaningful relationships in the classroom and beyond. When used properly, computers and other media are not tools to distract children. They are not held out as rewards for "good" behavior. They are not used in place of hands-on learning with natural or repurposed materials. They do not replace face-to-face communication or real social interaction.

Families should be aware of the latest research demonstrating the harmful consequences of the misuse of technology and media in an early learning environment, including:

• Language delays

- Physical, behavioral, and mental health problems
- Obesity
- Poor sleep
- Aggressive behavior
- Attention deficits
- Less reading
- Less creative play
- Gaps in social/emotional learning

Accordingly, families should not discard an early childhood education program merely because it does not offer the latest, greatest technological devices. Indeed, some of the very best early childhood education programs do not have "screens" at all, either by virtue of instructional design or lack of resources. They foster relationship-building skills with the use of other materials, and show tremendous benefits for children.

On the other hand, computers, screens, interactive media, and other communication devices are not going away. They are a part of every child's life. Children spend an average of seven hours a day using some form of screen media. Therefore, the key is to find an early childhood education program that uses technology as one of many methods to support children as they develop meaningful and real relationships in the environment.

Programs that use social constructivist or guided play-based approaches to early education recognize the uses and abuses of technology. They try to strike the proper balance. In these programs, educators guide children to use media as a vehicle to forge meaningful personal connections.

One such program that has developed best practices for the use of technology in the early learning environment is the HighScope program. That leading, research-based program has created a model position statement on the proper use of technology in early childhood education programs. The foundation for that position statement is the principle that technology, when appropriately designed for early learners and used under the skillful guidance of adults, can become an effective teaching tool. In fact, for some children with diverse learning styles, integrating technology in an intentional way can help them be successful. For example, a child with fine motor delay may benefit from use of a keyboard. Moreover, children identified as having special needs may require the use of assistive technology to support their learning in an inclusive environment.

Based on the HighScope position statement and our best available research, families should carefully consider only those early childhood education programs that demonstrate the following appropriate uses of technology:

- The use of technology is only a choice, not a necessity, because early learning occurs through real, human interaction.

- Technology is only one of many tools or materials that children may choose to use to share ideas, engage in role-playing, solve problems, and collaborate with others.
- Technology is used in moderation, only to supplement—not to replace—real materials that allow children to experience the world through all of their senses.
- Technology should never be an end in itself, or the "content" of any lesson plan or direct instruction.
- Media use must be interactive—promoting discovery, innovation, creativity, and reflection.
- Technology should spark collaboration, not isolation.
- Children should grow to use technology as another method of expressing themselves, sharing their ideas, and documenting their learning.
- Educators should be among the children, as partners in learning, when children use technology.
- Educators should work with children to use various forms of technology (e.g., audio, still, and video recording) as ways to make their learning visible.

Families should question any school that does not exhibit these best practices. The use of televisions in child care programs, for example, does not support learning and should be viewed as a red flag. However, families should consider programs in which educators inspire children to explore various forms of interactive media as a way to connect with others or to engage in research.

Howard Gardner has noted: "There has never been more material (or digital media) for teachers to present and for students to master in school. But at the end of the day, the most important questions are: What kind of human beings will we become? And, what kind of society will we have?" Inspired by this awareness, and by a study of schools of Reggio Emilia, Italy, two early childhood institutions with deep roots in the progressive movement, Winnetka Public School Nursery and Northwestern University Settlement House Head Start Preschool, created emergent curricula around a shared studio art teacher (*atelierista*). Encouraged by a collaborative team of professional educators, children worked on extended joint creative ventures that sprang from common interests. Through the "languages" of shared storytelling, sculpture and drawing, the power of shared documentation, and the technological wonder of Skype, a wider, more inclusive community was nurtured.

Chapter Seven

Will My Child Benefit from Special Education?

Everybody is a genius. But if you judge a fish by its ability to climb a tree, it will live its whole life believing it is stupid.
—Albert Einstein

Under a series of federal laws, including the Individuals with Disabilities Education Act (IDEA), Section 504 of the Rehabilitation Act, the Americans with Disabilities Act (ADA), the Head Start Act, and the Child Care and Development Block Grant Act (CCDBG), all children of preschool age who have an educational disability must receive free and appropriate special education services in the least restrictive educational environment

A. AVENUES THROUGH WHICH SPECIAL EDUCATION SERVICES MAY BE AVAILABLE TO YOUR CHILD

As declared by the U.S. Department of Education, the following federal laws require the appropriate inclusion of children with special needs within the regular education environment because of the overwhelming research indicating that such inclusion benefits all children:

1. The Individuals with Disabilities Education Act (IDEA)

Under IDEA, students with educational disabilities must be placed in an appropriate program of special education and related services. The IDEA expressly declares the congressional objective and philosophy that, whenever possible, students with educational disabilities should be "placed" in the same educational environment as children without educational disabilities:

55

"To the maximum extent appropriate, children with disabilities . . . [must be] educated with children who are not disabled."

Congress further provides that "removal of children with disabilities from the regular educational environment" may occur only when the "nature or severity of the disability of a child is such that education in regular classes with the use of supplementary aids and services cannot be achieved satisfactorily." The federal regulations implementing this statute make clear that school districts must strive to place a child in the "least restrictive environment" on a "continuum of alternative placements" from full inclusion in a regular classroom to the most restrictive residential placement.

The IDEA supports equality of opportunity and full participation for eligible children with disabilities birth through twenty-one by providing funds to states to assist them in developing and implementing systems of early intervention and special education and related services for all eligible infants, toddlers, children, and youth with disabilities.

The IDEA Part C program requires that eligible infants and toddlers with disabilities receive services in natural environments to the maximum extent appropriate, and the IDEA Part B program requires that eligible children with disabilities age three through twenty-one receive services in the least restrictive environment (LRE) to the maximum extent appropriate. Eligible children with disabilities under Part B of the IDEA are to receive the full range of supplementary aids and services to enable them to be educated with children who do not have disabilities, participate in the general educational or developmental curriculum, and participate in typical nonacademic activities with nondisabled peers, to the maximum extent appropriate.

2. Part C of IDEA

The Program for Infants and Toddlers with Disabilities (Part C of IDEA) requires states that receive Part C grants to develop and implement a statewide, comprehensive, coordinated, multidisciplinary, interagency system that provides early intervention services for infants and toddlers with disabilities from birth through age two, and to children with disabilities through age five (or until entry into kindergarten, whichever occurs earlier).

Appropriate early intervention services for any infant or toddler with a disability are to be provided in natural environments, including the home, and community settings in which children without disabilities participate, to the maximum extent appropriate, as determined by the individualized family service plan (IFSP) team.

The IDEA requires that the IFSP include a determination of the appropriate setting for providing early intervention services to an infant or toddler with a disability, including any justification for not providing a particular early intervention service in the natural environment. The IFSP team, which includes the parent and other team members, makes this determination, which must be consistent with the intended outcomes expected to be achieved by the child as written in the IFSP.

3. Part B, Section 619 of IDEA

The Preschool Grants Program (Part B, section 619 of the IDEA) provides formula grants to assist states to provide special education and related services to children with disabilities aged three through five. In order to be eligible for these grants, states must make a free appropriate public education (FAPE) available to all eligible children with disabilities ages three through five. These special education and related services must be provided, to the maximum extent appropriate, in the LRE based on each individual child's unique strengths and needs. It further requires that a continuum of placement options be available to best meet the diverse needs of children with disabilities.

The LRE requirements of the IDEA state a strong preference for educating children with disabilities in general education settings alongside their peers without disabilities to the maximum extent appropriate. Under LRE requirements, the IDEA presumes that the first placement option considered for each child with a disability is the regular classroom the child would attend if he or she did not have a disability, with appropriate supplementary aids and services.

Thus, before a child with a disability can be placed outside of the regular educational environment, the full range of supplementary aids and services that could be provided to facilitate the child's placement in the regular classroom setting must be considered. In addition, IDEA regulations specify that a child with a disability not be removed from education in age-appropriate regular classrooms solely because of needed modifications in the general education curriculum.

In 2012, the Office of Special Education Programs (OSEP), Office of Special Education and Rehabilitative Services, U.S. Department of Education issued a Dear Colleague Letter reiterating that IDEA and LRE requirements apply to preschool children with disabilities. Each local educational agency (LEA) must ensure that FAPE is provided in the LRE in which a child's unique needs can be met whether or not the LEA operates a public general early childhood program.

An LEA may provide special education and related services to a preschool child with a disability in a variety of settings, including their local public preschool program, if the LEA operates one, or, if the LEA does not operate a public program, other community-based settings, such as Head Start or community-based child care programs.

The letter states:

LEAs that do not have a public preschool program that can provide all the appropriate services and supports for a particular child with a disability must explore alternative methods to ensure the LRE requirements are met for that child. These methods may include: (1) providing opportunities for the participation of preschool children with disabilities in preschool programs operated by public agencies other than LEAs (such as Head Start or community-based child care); (2) enrolling preschool children with disabilities in private preschool programs for nondisabled preschool children; (3) locating classes for preschool children with disabilities in regular elementary schools; or providing home-based services. If a public agency determines that placement in a private preschool program is necessary for a child to receive FAPE, the public agency must make that program available at no cost to the parent.

4. Section 504 of the Rehabilitation Act of 1973

Section 504 of the Rehabilitation Act of 1973 prohibits discrimination on the basis of disability in public and private programs or activities that receive federal funds. This includes the responsibility to ensure that aids, benefits, or services are provided in the most integrated setting appropriate to the person's needs. Section 504 applies to public or private preschools, childcare centers, Head Start/Early Head Start programs, or family childcare homes that receive federal funds either directly or through a grant, loan, or contract.

5. Americans with Disabilities Act (ADA)

The Americans with Disabilities Act (ADA) protects individuals with disabilities from discrimination based on disability by public entities and public accommodations. Public entities and public accommodations include public or private early childhood programs such as family- or center-based childcare programs, public or private nursery schools, preschools, and also Head Start and Early Head Start programs run by public or nonpublic agencies.

In general, the ADA requires that childcare providers not discriminate against persons with disabilities on the basis of disability. They must provide children and parents with disabilities with an equal opportunity to participate in and benefit from the childcare center's services, programs, or activities, regardless of whether they receive federal funds. The ADA also requires that public entities and public accommodations provide their services, programs, or activities in the most integrated setting appropriate to the needs of the individual with a disability.

Young children in public settings, such as Head Start programs, operated by public entities are covered by Title II of ADA, which prohibits disability discrimination by state and local governmental entities, regardless of whether they receive federal funds. Young children in most private programs, including small family childcare programs, are covered by Title III of ADA, which prohibits disability discrimination by public accommodations, regardless of whether or not they receive federal funds.

6. Head Start Act

Head Start promotes the educational development of young children from low-income families and supports the mental, social, and emotional development of children from birth to age five. In addition to educational services, programs provide children and their families with comprehensive services including health, mental health, dental, nutrition, social, and other services. Head Start services are responsive to each child and family's cultural and linguistic heritage. Since 1972, Head Start has required that at least 10 percent of its enrollment opportunities are available to children with disabilities. Head Start and Early Head Start have exceeded this mandate and serve children in inclusive, developmentally appropriate programs.

7. Child Care and Development Block Grant Act (CCDBG)

The CCDBG Act of 2014 requires states to develop strategies for increasing the supply and quality of childcare services for children with disabilities. In addition, states must describe how they will coordinate their childcare services with other services for young children with disabilities operating at the federal, state, and local levels, including services under Part C and Part B, section 619 of the IDEA. The law also allows states to use funds reserved to improve the quality of childcare on professional development opportunities and specialized training on serving children with disabilities and their families.

B. WHAT STEPS SHOULD YOU TAKE TO DETERMINE WHETHER YOUR PRESCHOOL CHILD IS ELIGIBLE FOR SPECIAL EDUCATION SERVICES?

There are two primary ways in which children are identified as needing special education and related services: referral by a caregiver or educator, or by the child find process.

1. The Decision to Seek an Evaluation and Referral

All children have strengths. There is a wonderful diversity among children in how they experience the world and communicate with others. The variety of methods of cognition is sometimes referred to as neuro-diversity. Some children who experience the world and communicate with others in ways that are not typical experience tremendous obstacles from the educational system.

That system generally supports typically developing children, and does not accommodate neuro-diversity.

As a parent or caregiver, you know your child best. If you think your child needs help based on your observations of the way in which he or she plays, learns, speaks, acts, or moves, you should talk to your child's doctor and share your concerns.

The American Academy of Pediatrics recommends that children be screened for general development at nine, eighteen, and twenty-four or thirty months and for autism at eighteen and twenty-four months, or whenever a parent or provider has a concern. If you or the doctor thinks there might be a need for further evaluation, ask the doctor for a referral to a specialist who can do a more in-depth evaluation of your child.

Doctors your child might be referred to include:

- Developmental pediatricians. These doctors have special training in child development and children with special needs.
- Child neurologists. These doctors work on the brain, spine, and nerves.
- Child psychologists or psychiatrists. These doctors know about the human mind.
- Occupational therapists (OTs). These professionals help to develop strategies that allow a child to succeed in his or her home and school environment.

At the same time you ask the doctor for a referral to a specialist, you should call your state's public early childhood system to request a free evaluation to find out if your child qualifies for intervention services. You do not need to wait for a doctor's referral or a medical diagnosis to make this call. Where to call for a free evaluation from the state depends on your child's age:

- If your child is younger than three years old, contact your local early intervention system. Find your state's early intervention contact information at http://www.cdc.gov/ncbddd/actearly/parents/states.html.
- If your child is three years old or older, contact your local public school system. Even if your child is not old enough for kindergarten or enrolled in a public school, call your local elementary school or board of education and ask to speak with someone who can help you have your child evaluated.

In order to ensure that all children are able to realize their capacities, educational institutions must by law provide special education and related services to those children who have special needs, including those with diverse cognitive, physical, emotional, health, or development needs. Those needs, which exist along a continuum, include:

* *Developmental Disabilities*: a child with a developmental disability may grow and develop more slowly than other children. His or her physical, mental, or emotional development may be affected.
* *Emotional or Behavioral Needs*: this child may need help learning to follow daily routines or relating to others.
* *Exceptional Health Needs*: children may require specialized care due to conditions such as allergies, asthma, diabetes, epilepsy, sickle cell anemia, or because of a serious illness.
* *Hearing Impairment*: a child may have a mild or significant hearing impairment or may be deaf.
* *Language Skills (Communication Disorder)*: a child may have difficulty speaking or understanding speech. Expressing his or her needs or understanding rules and instructions may be difficult and frustrating for the child.
* *Learning Disability*: children learn in different ways, but some may need specialized care.
* *Physical Disability*: a child may have limited movement or require adaptive equipment, such as braces, a walker, or a wheelchair.
* *Vision Impairment*: a child may have a mild or significant vision impairment or may be blind.

If you believe that your child may have an educational disability, it is very important to get help as soon as possible. The earlier intervention is started, the more likely it is that your child will benefit from available services.

2. The Child Find Process: The School District's Obligation to Identify Children in Need of Special Education Services

The IDEA also requires states to adopt what is called a "child find" process. A child find process is designed to identify and refer children who may have a disability or are "at risk" to that state's early intervention (EI) program. Schools are required to locate, identify, and evaluate all children with disabilities from birth through age twenty-one. The child find mandate applies to all children who reside within a state, including children who attend private schools and public schools, highly mobile children, migrant children, homeless children, and children who are wards of the state.

In keeping with this federal law, each state has established its own early childhood intervention policies. Families should contact their state's particular education agency to find out about their state's specific policies. But all state share the following common ingredients in their required child find process:

- *Identification of Child Find Population*: The state determines which children are eligible for help.
- *Public Awareness*: The state raises awareness about children who may need special education services. The "public" includes stakeholders such as parents, caregivers, educators, school administrators, and physicians.
- *Referral and Intake*: A child is referred for services, in accordance with specific state-by-state procedures.
- *Identification*: The child is evaluated for possible disabilities or developmental delays.
- *Eligibility Determination*: Results of the evaluation of a child are compared to the state's eligibility guidelines, which must satisfy federal regulations.
- *Tracking and Monitoring*: The state provides a reliable method of monitoring children who are receiving services.
- *Interagency Coordination*: In those states in which many agencies collaborate to provide services required by IDEA, the agencies must combine resources to guarantee the availability of services.

Under the requirements of federal law, therefore, each public school district also must locate, identify, and evaluate all children with disabilities who are enrolled by their parents in private, including religious, elementary schools and secondary schools located in the school district. The public school district must develop and implement a plan to provide special education services for each child with a disability, including those children ages three to five.

Moreover, the public school district must also identify and provide services for children who are enrolled in private programs. The district must initiate and conduct meetings to develop, review, and revise a services plan for a child designated to receive services. The district must ensure that a representative of the religious or other private school attends each meeting where the child's needs or services are addressed. The services plan must describe the specific special education and related services that the school district will provide to the child.

3. Partnering with Your School to Develop and Implement an Individualized Education Program

An "Individualized Education Program" or IEP is a written statement for a child with a disability that is developed, reviewed, and revised. An Individual Education Program is a student's "curriculum" for the year, matching up the child's needs with an individualized, appropriate program. An IEP informs the parents of the measures the school district will take to assist the child in meeting the child's annual goals. The IEP is thus a legal obligation by the school to the child for whom the IEP is written. After a child is determined eligible for special education services, a team of school professionals and parents must meet within thirty calendar days to write an IEP.

a. Who Is Involved in the IEP?

The following stakeholders typically meet at the school district's office or at the child's school to develop an IEP: (1) the child's parents and/or legal guardians (if they choose not to attend then the school district must record attempts to have the parent(s) participate); (2) if parents cannot be located, surrogate parents must be appointed; (3) the child's special education teacher; (4) the child's regular education teacher (if the child is or may be participating in regular education); (5) the child (when appropriate); (6) a representative of the Local Education Agency or school district (i.e., case manager, principal, or assistant principal); (7) an individual who can interpret the instructional implications of evaluation results; and (8) at the discretion of the parent or school district, other individuals who have special knowledge or expertise regarding the child (i.e., related service personnel), including an independent school psychologist and a lawyer.

b. Who Gets an IEP?

For children under age three with disabilities, an Individualized Family Service Plan may serve as the IEP. Children ages three through twenty-two with disabilities who are determined eligible to receive an IEP must receive one.

c. What Must an IEP Include?

The IEP must include the following: a statement of the child's present level of functioning and educational performance; a statement of how the child's disability affects the child's involvement in the general education curriculum and participation in appropriate activities; a statement of the measurable annual goals, including benchmarks (short-term objectives); a statement of the special education, related services, supplementary aids, program modifications, and supports to be provided to the child, including the projected starting date, along with the frequency, location, and duration of the services; an explanation of the extent the child with disabilities will not be participating with nondisabled children in the regular education classroom; a statement of the modifications required for the child to participate in state or district achievement assessments, if appropriate; a statement of how the child's progress toward the annual goals will be measured, and a statement of how the child's parent will be regularly informed; and a statement of needed postsecondary school transition services.

The IEP also contains a declaration of special factors to be considered in meeting the educational needs of the child, including:

1. positive behavioral interventions, strategies, and supports to address a child whose behavior impedes his or her learning
2. the language needs of the child, particularly limited-English-proficiency students
3. appropriate instruction and use of Braille for blind or visually impaired children
4. communication needs, particularly of children who are deaf or hard of hearing
5. assistive technology devices and services for children when deemed necessary and appropriate by the IEP team

d. What "Related Services" Must the District Provide?

The district must also provide related services such as transportation; speech and language services; audiology services; counseling services; social work services; physical or occupational therapy; related medical services for diagnosis, evaluation, and consultation; interpreters; special reader services; braillists and typists; transition services; and vocational services and vocational programs.

e. How Is an IEP Effectively Monitored?

At least annually, the child's IEP and placement must be monitored. The child's benchmarks and short-term objectives should be monitored quarterly. Parents should be kept aware of the child's progress. Reports of pupil progress must be given at a rate that is at least equivalent to that given to children without educational disabilities (i.e., quarterly, with progress reports and report cards).

f. How Can the IEP Process Be Managed to Reduce Conflict?

The IEP process is often characterized by tension and conflict between the parents of a child with special educational needs and the school district. From the perspective of the parent or guardian, the process is emotionally difficult because it involves a disability in a child. That emotional strain often manifests itself in aggression toward the district and its professionals. In particular, parents may become assertive in their demand for individual services. This tension may be exacerbated if the parents have brought with them to the IEP meeting a legal or educational expert.

From the district's point of view, the provision of effective special education services can be extremely expensive. The administrators charged with monitoring the IEP process are often viewed by the school district as "gatekeepers." That label suggests that the school district's representatives in the process may bring with them a strong desire to contain costs. The district's motive to reduce costs is often incompatible with a parent's desire to obtain effective services for a child.

There are two ways to reduce this inherently tense situation. First, the district must provide the parents with sincere communication regarding the process. The communication must be clear, nonpatronizing, nonthreatening, and honest. The tone of the administrators and educational professionals is vital. It must be conciliatory, and it must manifest a genuine interest in serving the educational needs of the child.

As part of this communication, the district must also allow parents time to reflect on the IEP documents and on the dialogue at the IEP meetings. All too often, districts try to get parents to sign off on an IEP plan for their children on the spot, right in the middle of a first meeting. This is simply unfair and will breed disharmony down the road.

Second, the district must make sure that at least one of its educational professionals involved in the IEP process really knows the child. Because special education tends to be separated administratively from "regular education," it is not unusual for a district's IEP representative to have had absolutely no contact with the child involved. Not only do parents justifiably resent the presence of district administrators who do not understand the needs of their children, these administrators have no ability to contribute to a legitimate educational plan for the child. As such, administrators who do not understand the child tend to fight for the district's cost saving goal rather than for the educational needs of the child. That approach, in turn, creates tremendous hostility among parents at the IEP meetings and throughout the process.

g. The Limits of Appropriate Discipline for Children with Disabilities

A student with disabilities may not be expelled or suspended for longer than ten days for behavior or a condition that is a "manifestation" of his or her disability. If the behavior is not a result of the student's disability, however, the child can be disciplined in accordance with the district's discipline policy.

A school district may remove a student with disabilities from school for up to ten days, under circumstances that would allow the school to remove a nondisabled child. If the disabled child has been removed from school for more than ten cumulative days in a school term, services must be provided to the extent necessary to assist the student in progressing in the general curriculum and achieving the IEP goals.

"Changes in placement" require a case-by-case determination that the change is necessary, as well as the development of a behavioral assessment plan or review of a student's current behavior assessment plan, within ten business days; notification to the parent(s); and an alternative free appropriate public education (FAPE).

A "change in placement" is appropriate *only* if a child carries a weapon to school or a school function, or knowingly possesses or uses illegal drugs or sells or solicits controlled substances at school or a school function. A change of placement to an appropriate alternative education setting is necessary and acceptable, for the same amount of time as would be endured by a nondisabled student, but no more than forty-five days.

Alternatively, a district may effect a change in placement pursuant to the ruling of a hearing examiner. In an expedited due process hearing, a hearing officer may order an appropriate interim alternative education setting for up to forty-five days if the hearing officer finds that injury to the student or others may result from the current placement. With regard to appropriate interim alternative placements, the IEP determines the propriety of the alternative placement, and the student must remain in that placement pending review by the hearing officer.

Moreover, the alternative interim placement must enable the student to continue in the general curriculum, enable the student to continue to receive required services and modifications, including those in the student's IEP, and provide services and modifications addressing the student's behavior and focusing on prevention of the behavior's reoccurrence.

In determining whether and how to discipline a particular child with special needs, the school district and its personnel should consider the student's physical freedom and social interaction. The district should administer behavior interventions that respect human dignity and personal privacy and ensure the student's right to the least restrictive environment.

In order to establish institutional guarantees of appropriate disciplinary procedures, the school should establish and maintain a committee to develop policies and procedures regarding the proper use of behavioral interventions. The school's policies and procedures regarding the use of behavioral interventions must comply with the state board of education's rules. The school's policies and procedures also should be developed with advice from parents of regular and special education students, teachers, administrators, advocates, and experts in the field of behavior intervention. The practices should emphasize positive intervention, incorporate generally accepted behavior interventions in the field, include determination criteria, and include effective, but nonintrusive, monitoring procedures.

C. THE BENEFITS TO ALL CHILDREN OF SPECIAL EDUCATION INCLUSION

Children with special needs or "special rights," as they are referred to in Reggio Emilia, should be fully included in the classroom and not defined by whatever limitations some may perceive them to have. Instead, they should be welcomed and respected for their capability to use all of their senses to learn. Children with special needs and any other children with visible differences may spark incredible opportunities for learning in an environment with young children, especially, and are celebrated for adding diversity to the learning environment.

Chapter Eight

Should I Consider the Advantages of a Dual-Language Program?

What we want is to see the child in pursuit of knowledge, and not knowledge
in pursuit of the child.
—George Bernard Shaw

The best early learning environments for all children are early childhood
education programs that value and support each child's home language. They
are best for children for whom English is an additional language, and they are
best for children for whom English is their home language.

In the Foundation for Child Development's report titled "PreK–3rd: Challenging Common Myths about Young Dual Language Learners: An Update
to the Seminal 2008 Report," Linda M. Espinosa presents a wealth of research demonstrating best practices in the early education of children for
whom English is an additional language.

According to that research, there has been a dramatic increase in the
number of dual language learners (DLL) and in the variety of languages
spoken by children and their families in early childhood education programs
throughout the country. Head Start, for example, has documented more than
140 different languages among their families enrolled, with approximately
30 percent of all children identified as dual-language learners.

Parents and program administrators might be tempted to think that these
children need an early education program designed to immerse them only in
English. After all, it would seem that children could be overwhelmed by
having to learn two languages in the early years and that the best way for
them to acquire English quickly is by total immersion in that single language.
Moreover, because early childhood education programs usually do not have
the capacity to teach in multiple languages, it also appears that such pro-

grams would naturally decide to provide instruction only in the common language of English.

Yet these assumptions about the early education of dual-language learners are simply false. As the Foundation for Child Development has found: "With such a daunting challenge facing our educators, it seems reasonable to expect most programs will implement English-only instructional approaches. While reasonable, this would be a misguided conclusion."

Rather, as the Foundation for Child Development recognizes, the research makes it clear that "children need frequent and intentional support for the home language while they are acquiring English in order to benefit academically, socially, and cognitively from their emergent bilingualism." The most recent evidence suggests that support for the home language during the pre-kindergarten years will help, not hurt, long-term attainment in English.

According to the Foundation for Child Development:

> Conclusions from the current science suggest that young DLL children are quite capable of learning academic content in two languages. In fact, they benefit cognitively from learning more than one language. Transitioning to English too soon may cost them in the long run, and many early literacy skills learned in the home language transfer to English.

English can and should be successfully introduced in early childhood education programs. But if English completely replaces a child's home language, and a child does not have the opportunity to continue to learn in that familiar language, the child's linguistic, conceptual, and academic development will be at risk. Exposure to English during early childhood combined with ongoing opportunities to learn important concepts in the home language results in the highest achievement in both the home language and in English.

Far from diminishing the child's home language, therefore, an early childhood education program's teachers and administrators should actively encourage families to continue to talk with, read to, sing to, and use the home language in everyday activities. Those home language connections will promote continued development of children's first language while they are also acquiring English in their pre-K settings.

Families of dual-language learners should look for an early childhood education environment that celebrates the different home languages of children. In such an environment:

- Teachers and school administrators meet early and throughout the year with families, and where possible conduct home visits.
- The classroom is filled with pictures and other media that display the languages, cultures, and practices of the children in the learning community.

- Books and other materials represent the languages and cultures of the children in the classroom. They are regularly read aloud by the teacher with help from the children or the children's family.
- The child, the teacher, a caregiver, or a community volunteer introduces vocabulary words and phrases in a child's home language.
- Stories from different cultures are told, read, and acted in different languages.
- Songs are sung in different languages.
- Common words and concepts are articulated in both English and in home languages as a bridge to understanding.
- Materials are labeled in multiple languages as ways to help children make connections.
- Children help each other to understand their different languages.
- Meaningful relationships are developed between the school and extended family members to gain an understanding of family expectations for their children's development and learning.
- Family partnerships that are mutually respectful, engage in two-way communication, and incorporate important cultural and family background information offer promise for stronger home-school connections.

This language-rich early learning environment benefits all children, including those whose home language is English. Some native English families may believe that their children would not be sufficiently challenged to learn literacy in an environment in which other languages are embraced. But that belief is unfounded.

The evidence is overwhelming. An early learning environment that includes and celebrates dual language learners along with native English speakers is an effective model for both DLL students *and* native English speakers. As the Foundation for Child Development reports, all children "benefit cognitively, linguistically, culturally, and economically from learning more than one language."

Accordingly, all families should seek out an early childhood education program that not only includes children for whom English is an additional language but also embraces the home languages of those children.

Chapter Nine

Should I Consider the Advantages of a Program That Embraces Diversity?

Teach the children so it will not be necessary to teach the adults.
—Abraham Lincoln

Diversity is a source of great strength in an early childhood education program. Diverse early learning environments help all children to learn, and to become healthy and productive citizens.

A. DIVERSE EARLY LEARNING ENVIRONMENTS HELP ALL CHILDREN LEARN

A diverse learning environment actually helps children strengthen their cognitive abilities. We now know that children learn best in small groups. And we also know that the groups that are best for learning are those that are diverse.

When a child is exposed to different thoughts, ideas, perspectives, and backgrounds, the child experiences cognitive dissonance, incongruity, and imbalance. The child's brain then must work hard to process the information, absorb the dissonance, and to accommodate the unusual perspective. Regular encounters with children with diverse experiences strengthen a child's brain. They help to develop the child's mental capacity to engage in higher-order thinking skills and complex problem-solving strategies.

A diverse early learning environment also builds a child's critical cognitive capacity to take another person's perspective. The ability to appreciate, understand, and respect the thoughts, feelings, and intentions of different children is quite challenging. The challenge is greater when the child seems

73

to be different. But the pattern of confronting and overcoming the challenge of accommodating different perspectives is the key to learning. The experience enables the child to embrace rather than fear difference.

Children who fear difference because they have not had the opportunity to experience it may develop a profound hostility to difference throughout their lives. That hostility can manifest itself in bullying and violence.

Children who learn to embrace difference at an early age, by contrast, are more likely to be healthy and stable adults. They have learned that if their own view of the world is ruptured by an unusual experience, they have the ability to repair that rupture. The rhythm of rupture followed by repair in a child's brain helps that child to persevere and focus, and to develop focus and perseverance in all of their activities. In other words, a diverse learning environment builds executive function.

Our best evidence demonstrates the remarkable educational benefits that all children receive from a diverse learning environment, including:

- Diverse learning environments provide benefits for all students, including improved academic achievement, critical thinking, collaboration, and communication skills.
- All students who attend racially diverse schools grow to achieve higher standardized test scores and are more likely to graduate from college than those who do not.
- Diversity promotes better problem solving.
- Diverse groups of learners consistently outperform otherwise high-achieving groups in solving complex problems.
- Diverse individuals in a group create a higher level of collective intelligence than groups comprised even of higher-achieving individuals.
- Diversity produces an increase in the academic capabilities of individuals of all races.
- Diversity in the early learning environment fosters increased individual and group innovation.
- Children who learn math in a diverse learning environment do better than children who learn math in a homogeneous environment.
- Because children who have important relationships with diverse peers in an early-learning environment grow to manage bias, they do not suffer the interference with cognitive processes and executive function that such bias can produce in later life.

B. DIVERSE EARLY LEARNING ENVIRONMENTS HELP ALL CHILDREN BECOME HEALTHY AND PRODUCTIVE CITIZENS

Diverse early learning environments also promote cross-racial understanding; reduce prejudice, stereotyping, and implicit bias; and foster collaborative problem solving. These skills are vital to a child's ultimate ability to find success and well-being in increasingly diverse work and social environments.

In particular, the latest research demonstrates the many social benefits to all children of a diverse early learning environment, including:

- Children exposed to racially diverse peers in the classroom exhibit reduced adherence to racial stereotypes and reduced racial prejudice.
- Diverse learning environments help all children to reduce and to regulate the anxieties that might otherwise be created from novel inter-racial interactions.
- The body's learned ability to regulate anxieties and cardiac stress otherwise created by nonroutine inter-racial interactions is important to a child's long-term physical health.
- Inter-racial contact lowers harmful chemical stress responses in the body early in the development of a cross-racial friendship, and therefore such contact in the early years has substantial immediate and lasting value.
- Early interactions between diverse children reduce explicit biases (prejudicial attitudes that a person endorses at a conscious level) and implicit biases (prejudices in judgment and behavior that result from subtle subconscious cognitive processes) in the development of future interpersonal relationships.
- By engaging in early inter-racial contact, children experience less anxiety, increased empathy, and reduced urges to display the kind of social dominance that leads to bullying and violence against children who appear to be different.
- A diverse early learning environment creates vital cross-cultural competencies, including the ability to understand and navigate a culture different from one's own.
- Children who learn in a diverse learning environment grow to be professionals with the cross-cultural competency necessary to compete in a diverse global economy.
- Diversity produces greater democratic citizenship outcomes because children grow to understand that differences need not be divisive, to appreciate another person's perspective, and to become engaged in leadership and civic activities.
- A diverse early learning environment produces children who are better able to resolve conflict without violence.

- Inter-racial contact in the early years leads to stronger interpersonal cognitive skills in general because children learn to be more careful, nuanced, and precise in their perceptions of the thoughts, feelings, and intentions of others.
- The lack of diversity facilitates the growth in minority students of stereotype threat, which is a powerful force undermining belief in one's own abilities.
- Diverse early educational environments help to mitigate the harmful effects of implicit bias in all children, particularly nonminority children.

As the research also indicates, children who experience a diverse learning environment in their early years derive the most profound and lasting educational and social benefits. Inter-racial contact in a child's formative years is far more effective in promoting the many benefits of diversity than intermittent inter-racial contact and even substantial adult inter-racial contact. In fact, the development of early educational environments in which children of different races form meaningful relationships is far more effective at promoting the benefits of diversity than any other method of teaching.

Chapter Ten

How Can I Make Sense of Formal Measures of Quality and Ratings by Accrediting Bodies?

Not everything that can be counted counts, and not everything that counts can be counted.
—Albert Einstein

Families who wish to consider formal measures of quality may research individual programs to determine whether they are: (1) accredited by a professional organization; (2) aligned with a state's particular early learning standards; or (3) display exceptional attributes of quality.

A. ACCREDITATION

In addition to meeting the mandatory licensing requirements set forth in each state, early education providers may also voluntarily seek accreditation from a number of national organizations. To achieve accreditation, a provider must demonstrate a commitment to excellence that exceeds the minimum standards established in the licensing requirements.

The primary accreditors of center-based preschools are: the National Association for the Education of Young Children (NAEYC), the National Early Childhood Program Accreditation (NECPA), and the National Accreditation Commission (NAC).

For in-home providers, the National Association for Family Child Care (NAFCC) offers accreditation that roughly parallels the process for center-based providers. In addition, the Council for Professional Recognition (CPR) accredits individual teachers.

While there is considerable overlap between these organizations and their assessment or accreditation processes, their unique aspects and individual missions deserve careful attention.

1. NAEYC

The National Association for the Education of Young Children (NAEYC) takes a broad-based view of accreditation. It evaluates candidate preschools based on the following ten standards:

- *Relationships*: The program promotes positive relationships among all children and adults to encourage each child's sense of individual worth and belonging as part of a community and to foster each child's ability to contribute as a responsible community member.
- *Curriculum*: The program implements a curriculum that is consistent with its goals for children and promotes learning and development in each of the following areas: social, emotional, physical, language, and cognitive.
- *Teaching*: The program uses developmentally, culturally, and linguistically appropriate and effective teaching approaches that enhance each child's learning and development in the context of the program's curriculum goals.
- *Assessment of Child Progress*: The program is informed by ongoing systematic, formal, and informal assessment approaches to provide information on children's learning and development. These assessments occur within the context of reciprocal communications with families and with sensitivity to the cultural contexts in which children develop. Assessment results are used to benefit children by informing sound decisions about children, teaching, and program improvement.
- *Health*: The program promotes the nutrition and health of children and protects children and staff from illness and injury.
- *Teachers*: The program employs and supports a teaching staff that has the educational qualifications, knowledge, and professional commitment necessary to promote children's learning and development and to support families' diverse needs and interests.
- *Families*: The program establishes and maintains collaborative relationships with each child's family to foster children's development in all settings. These relationships are sensitive to family composition, language, and culture.
- *Community Relationships*: The program establishes relationships with and uses the resources of the children's communities to support the achievement of program goals.
- *Physical Environment*: The program has a safe and healthful environment that provides appropriate and well-maintained indoor and outdoor physi-

cal environments. The environment includes facilities, equipment, and materials to facilitate child and staff learning and development.

- *Leadership and Management*: The program effectively implements policies, procedures, and systems that support stable staff and strong personnel, fiscal, and program management so all children, families, and staff have high-quality experiences.

Guided by these ten standards, NAEYC requires early education providers to comply with an exhaustive list of individual requirements and best practices. NAEYC does not evaluate each benchmark at every candidate preschool; however, compliance with some benchmarks (such as the total absence of corporal punishment) are mandatory for accreditation.

Due to its relative seniority in the field and its highly detailed criteria, NAEYC has established itself as the preeminent early childhood education organization in the nation. Many other accreditors have followed the model established by NAEYC.

2. NECPA

The National Early Childhood Program Accreditation (NECPA) offers an alternate route for providers who would like to receive outside recognition but do not want to undertake the NAEYC process. NECPA requires candidate preschools to engage in a detailed self-study in advance of a "verification" visit—in which a NECPA inspector observes the program in its day-to-day operation. This process takes roughly one year. If and when a preschool is approved, its accreditation term lasts three years until it must be renewed.

Established in 1991, NECPA markets itself as the only "independent" accrediting body; yet it readily admits the heavy influence of the NAEYC standards on its own process. In addition, it requires providers to register (i.e., pay a fee) before it releases its exact accreditation standards and guidelines.

3. NAC

The National Accreditation Commission (NAC) is another pathway to accreditation administered by the Association for Early Learning Leaders. Formerly known as the National Association of Child Care Providers (NACCP), the organization underwent a major "rebrand" in 2012. It divides its accreditation process into three steps.

First, an interested provider must embark upon a self-study. The time frame is left fairly open by NAC, and the study can range anywhere from six months to two years. Next, after the provider completes their self-study, NAC sends an inspector on a validation visit. Although NAC gives providers a two-week window, the exact time of the visit remains unannounced until the inspector arrives at the site. This helps ensure a more realistic impression of how the provider operates on a daily basis. Finally, following the validation visit, NAC reviews the inspector's findings and issues a recommendation.

NAC requires interested preschools to meet ninety-one standards spread across six categories: Administration, Family Engagement, Health and Safety, Curriculum, Interactions between Teacher and Student, and Classroom Health and Safety. Inspectors evaluate schools' compliance with these standards based on indicators that they are trained to find within the learning environment. NAC also has measures to ensure that accredited schools maintain compliance. It requires both annual reports and prompt notification of any major changes—such as the installation of a new program director. In addition, it retains the right to make an unannounced visit in order to test compliance. Failures or deficiencies in any area can lead to a program losing its NAC accreditation.

4. NAFCC

The National Association for Family Child Care accredits family providers rather than center-based programs. A "family provider" is an early childhood educator who operates a preschool or daycare facility out of his or her own home. Its accreditation process is fairly similar to that of NECPA, but adapted for the family provider context.

At the outset, the family provider undertakes a self-evaluation based on NAFCC quality standards. The NAFCC views the self-evaluation as a two-step process. First, the family provider must master the standards of quality. Then, the provider must compile and submit appropriate documentation to ensure that it meets all eligibility requirements; this includes providing proof of CPR and first-aid certification and submitting to a full and thorough background check. Before accrediting a family provider, NAFCC will send one of its specialists to observe the provider during a field visit. So long as the family provider maintains all applicable standards, accreditation need only be renewed every three years.

Like NECPA, NAFCC only releases its standards to providers after they enroll. For parents interested in finding a family provider for their child's preschool education, NAFCC accreditation is a reliable indicator of a safe and nurturing environment.

5. CPR

The Council for Professional Recognition (CPR) handles the process of certifying individual educators. It has developed several criteria for those seeking CPR accreditation.

Applicants must have at least a high school diploma or GED to begin the accreditation process. They must amass at least 120 hours of occupational development (training sessions); educators must have at least ten hours each in eight specific areas of development as part of this requirement. Applicants must prepare a "professional portfolio" containing references and other relevant information within six months of beginning the accreditation process.

Within three years of applying for accreditation, applicants must log at least 480 hours of hands-on fieldwork. In addition, all applicants must undergo observation by a CPR-certified evaluator during a verification visit. They must also pass a standardized Child Development Associate (CDA) exam. Once all materials are available for review, a CPR committee will scrutinize an applicant's file to determine if he or she has demonstrated sufficient competency to earn accreditation. While test and visit performance weigh heavily on the minds of the committee, CPR is quick to emphasize that the review of the file is a holistic one.

CPR prizes thirteen standards of competency tucked within the following six goals:

- To establish and maintain a safe, healthy learning environment
- To advance physical and intellectual competence
- To support social and emotional development and to provide positive guidance
- To establish positive and productive relationships with families
- To ensure a well-run, purposeful program responsive to participant needs
- To maintain a commitment to professionalism

The CPR standards for individual educators roughly parallel the NAEYC standards for center-based providers. NAEYC views CPR accreditation as a mark of excellence for an individual educator.

B. STATE BENCHMARKS AND EARLY LEARNING STANDARDS

1. State Quality Rating Systems

Several states have adopted quality-rating systems for licensed early childhood education programs in order to increase the availability of information regarding the quality of each program and to reward high-rated programs with financial support. States such as North Carolina, for example, have implemented a one-to-five-star rating system to help parents and policymakers gauge the effectiveness of the state's programs. To reach the highest rating of five stars, programs must allow trained, university-based observers to evaluate the programs using the Early Childhood Environment Rating Scale (E-CERS).

The E-CERS is one of four child-focused environment scales, and it evaluates a program's ability to provide high-quality care environments for children. The E-CERS assesses forty-three items organized into seven subcategories. These categories examine a program's physical spaces, basic care of children, activities, interactions, and structure, while also assessing children's language-reasoning and surveying parents and staff.

Like other environment rating scales, the E-CERS was developed to evaluate the "process quality" for children. Process quality refers to children's experiences within a childcare setting, including interactions, materials, and activities. The quality of the interactions in the educational environment, which is best measured through observation, has proven to be a better predictor of child outcomes than class-size ratios, group size, cost of care, and type of care.

Similarly, some states rely on the Program Administration Scale (PAS) to measure the leadership and management practices of early childhood programs. The PAS provides valuable information to directors about the quality of their administrative practices and can be used as a springboard for program improvement efforts. The PAS measures quality on a seven-point scale in twenty-five items clustered in ten subscales:

- Human Resources Development
- Personnel Cost and Allocation
- Center Operations
- Child Assessment
- Fiscal Management
- Program Planning and Evaluation
- Family Partnerships
- Marketing and Public Relations
- Technology
- Staff Qualifications

2. State Early Learning Standards

In addition, every state has developed and implemented early learning standards to guide students, parents, educators, and caregivers. The early learning standards in effect today range in length from a three-page brochure (West Virginia) to a three-volume book (California). Some emphasize achievement of tangible goals geared toward kindergarten readiness (Hawaii, Illinois), while others focus on the process through which children learn (Michigan, Minnesota). Still others, such as Oklahoma and Virginia, occupy a middle ground—often emphasizing the role of individual educators. The differences in these standards can have very real impacts on the nature of a child's experience.

This section describes the standards of four states: Oklahoma, Virginia, Illinois, and Michigan. These standards are offered as prime examples of the different approaches implemented by states throughout the country. If parents and caregivers would like to determine precisely where their state falls on the spectrum of early educational philosophies, the Early Learning Standards for all fifty states are readily available via an Internet search or accessible at http://nrckids.org/index.cfm/resources/state-licensing-and-regulation-information.

a. Oklahoma

Oklahoma has had great success in expanding access to quality prekindergarten education. In order to assess the effectiveness of its early education system, Oklahoma places special emphasis on the PASS (Priority Academic Student Skills) standards. For early learners, the PASS standards encompass nine skill areas or "domains."

While five of these nine domains measure growth in traditional academic areas such as Language Arts and Mathematics, Oklahoma has also developed four domains that provide more holistic indicators. The PASS standards attempt to measure Approaches to Learning, Creative Skills, Social and Personal Skills, and Health, Safety, and Physical Development. By highlighting these areas of growth, Oklahoma demonstrates its commitment to ensure that early learners develop positive, lifelong habits in addition to realizing more traditional academic goals.

Although Oklahoma has established certain focal points in its curriculum, it leaves considerable discretion to early childhood educators to determine how best to reach these broad goals. In other words, teachers construct the vehicle that helps early learners grow and develop using the PASS standards as a blueprint. The PASS document states, "Teachers trained in early childhood curriculum theories will provide an enriched curriculum including (the PASS standards) and many others." Oklahoma recognizes the critical role of individual educators and the need for flexibility and adaptability in order to best serve each child.

Coupled with the PASS standards, Oklahoma has also published benchmarks to measure the overall effectiveness of providers. The fingerprints of the social constructivist approach to education appear all over these benchmarks. Specifically, Oklahoma calls on its educators to provide active climates for learning that respect the cultural, language, and learning differences among the students. Oklahoma also recognizes the importance of documentation—the collection of information from multiple sources in order to better understand the child's needs. In sum, Oklahoma's early learning standards approach education as a process rather than simply as an end goal. It serves as a model for many other states in the realm of early childhood education.

b. Virginia

Virginia's "Foundation Blocks for Early Learning" opens with a quote from Nobel Laureate Dr. James Heckman: "Early childhood education fosters cognitive skills along with attentiveness, motivation, self-control, and the character skills that turn knowledge into know-how and people into productive citizens." Dr. Heckman's words and the use of the term *blocks* instead of *goals* convey Virginia's long-range approach to early childhood education. Virginia has developed its curriculum with an eye toward the future as much as the present.

Looking toward the children's more immediate future, many of Virginia's Foundation Blocks are geared toward kindergarten readiness. Similar to Oklahoma, the document recognizes the need for individual educators to adapt these broad principles to the needs of their classrooms. Its eight domains also mirror Oklahoma's organization of concepts, though with slightly different titles.

Virginia divides these eight domains into individual Foundation Blocks that highlight specific skills. Each block contains a list of suggested activities for educators to use in order to engage the children in developing these skills. For example, Science Foundation Block 8 ("Resources") highlights the importance of conservation and recycling. In order to teach this concept, the Foundation Block suggests children first learn to identify recyclable and nonrecyclable items. Children can then put their knowledge to practical use in a scavenger hunt around the learning environment to find recyclable items. After scrounging for materials, the class can establish a recycling center together. Led by a perceptive educator, a seemingly simple exercise in organizing materials can form lifelong habits that benefit both the students and the broader society.

Virginia's particular emphasis on activities demonstrates its appreciation for the benefits of active learning. It recognizes that children learn best when given freedom to explore and create. In this spirit, Virginia prefaces the Science Foundation Blocks by observing, "preschool children are born scientists, and nurturing their natural love of science is key." These words summarize not only Virginia's approach to science instruction but also its view of early childhood education as a whole. As such, the Foundation Blocks themselves build upon the instincts and lived experiences of preschoolers—

already considerable even at their young age. Together, these factors pave the way for success and continued growth in kindergarten and beyond.

c. Illinois

Illinois espouses a relatively more goal-based philosophy when compared to Oklahoma and Virginia. In fact, the state has developed thirty-two specific measurements for its early learners. While the Illinois standards are meant to be implemented as part of an overarching "standard of experience," the document prioritizes tangible, academic progress for young children.

The Illinois Early Learning Standards cover nine domains, of which eight are substantially the same as Oklahoma and Virginia. Illinois also has a unique domain titled "English Language Learner Home Language Development." Here, Illinois attempts to implement recent neuroscientific research that spotlights the ability of early learners to develop multiple languages at once.

Educators first solidify the child's home language rather than squeezing it out in favor of English. Once the early learner's native tongue is well established (usually by age three), the child can then apply her linguistic skills to English, fostering a smoother transition. After transitioning to English, the child can further expand competency and begin tackling goals across other areas of the curriculum.

In developing these standards, Illinois emphasizes uniformity with both its own K–12 Standards and the Common Core. It also aims for standardization across different classrooms; the document makes clear that it intends to implement a fairly homogeneous approach for teachers. Illinois—like some other states—has begun to recognize the critical importance of social and emotional learning, and thus has incorporated social and emotional goals into its early learning standards.

In its Guiding Principles, Illinois makes clear that it views early learners as competent and capable; children are willing and eager to learn. It also emphasizes that each child develops at his own unique rate. Thus, while the thirty-two goals are used as measuring sticks, Illinois certainly does not expect a child to master all areas. Instead, the Illinois Learning Standards provide a big-picture context against which the relative strengths and weaknesses of individual learners may be further explored.

d. Michigan

Michigan takes a comprehensive view of early childhood education by approaching the topic from two directions. It has combined its early learning expectations for children with its benchmarks for providers to create a single policy titled "Early Childhood Standards of Quality for Prekindergarten." It features nine domains for student progress along with seven areas of emphasis for providers.

Each of the nine domains is further divided into a number of subdomains. Within each of these subdomains, the Standards of Quality list a number of "Early Learning Expectations" coupled with "Emerging Indicators"—signals that help parents and educators see the children's progress. The expectations are not structured in a manner that implies a concrete, definite goal. Instead, they are tailored to stimulate the development of a habit or mindset. One Early Learning Expectation for Literacy is especially instructive. It reads, "Children *begin* to understand written language read to them from a variety of meaningful materials, using *reading-like* behaviors, and *make progress* toward *becoming* conventional readers (emphasis mine)."

In short, Michigan's standards measure the formation of habits rather than the achievement of goals. This approach—useful at any age and especially appropriate in the early learning environment—values the different attributes of the children, who are judged only based on their own personal progress and are not compared against each other.

Michigan's approach also is unusual in its celebration of a child's individuality. Providers are exhorted to "accept all children's individual levels of development, interest, temperament, cultural background, language, and learning styles and use them as the basis of planning the program." On a similar note, providers must "assure an environment where no child is mocked, belittled, bullied, or ignored."

Statements such as these, coupled with an abiding respect for diversity, abound throughout the Standards of Quality. Underlying these directives is a clear belief in the importance of building a community of learners that enables each child to more fully grasp his or her potential. Michigan's Standards of Quality call on preschools to teach children how to live in a diverse, pluralistic society. Seen in this light, preschools are classrooms of democracy.

e. Indicators of Exceptional Quality

In addition to determining whether a particular pre-K provider meets a state's standards or is accredited by a respected organization, families should consider whether that provider demonstrates the indicators of exceptional quality established by NIEER and by the experience of Reggio-inspired programs.

i. NIEER

An initiative of Rutgers University, NIEER does not participate in any accreditation processes for individual early learning environments. What NIEER does offer is a wealth of research and resources to benefit educators, administrators, and parents.

As a clearinghouse of high-quality information concerning early childhood education, NIEER is unparalleled. Its annual yearbook, "The State of Preschool," offers a state-by-state breakdown of key indicators relating to early childhood education access and quality. Parents will find its concise, digestible format both very helpful in its own right as well as an excellent starting point for any further information they desire.

NIEER also provides ten benchmarks of a high-quality pre-K program that parents can use in assessing the programs they are considering:

- Early learning standards: comprehensive
- Teacher degree: BA
- Teacher specialized training: specializing in pre-K
- Assistant teacher degree: CDA or equivalent
- Teacher in-service: at least fifteen hours per year
- Maximum class size for three- and four-year-olds: twenty or lower
- Staff-child ratio for three- and four-year-olds: 1:10 or better
- Screening/referral: health; and at least one support service
- Meals: at least one per day
- Monitoring: site visits at least every five years

ii. Meeting the Reggio Emilia Gold Standard

A truly Reggio-inspired social constructivist early learning program will readily satisfy important NAEYC standards, as well as the NIEER benchmarks. Furthermore, a Reggio-inspired social constructivist learning environment will significantly exceed the NAEYC and NIEER standards. Parents determine if a program has created a Reggio-inspired social constructivist learning environment by observing whether that environment reflects the following truly "democratic" qualities:

D ocumentation—the program deepens and makes visible individual and community learning through many forms of media.

E mergent and negotiated curriculum—the program does not have a canned or standardized curriculum, but rather encourages teachers to guide the development of essential math, literacy, and scientific competencies in a respectful relationship with their students.

M ultiple representations are valued—the program inspires children to express themselves in many different ways.

O ne hundred languages of children are supported—the program respects the multiple forms of communication that children engage in.

C ollaboration is modeled and encouraged—the program engages children in small and large group projects and shared activities, and its educational professionals model collaboration in all of their interactions with each other and with families.

R esearch about learning is performed by teachers, families, and students—the program recognizes that teachers and families are partners with their children in the learning process.

A telier integrates creative expression into all learning—the program, ideally with the support of an art studio and an art studio teacher, includes many forms of artistic expression as a vital part of all of the learning.

T ime for exploration is not artificially limited—the program does not set arbitrary time constraints on children who seek to explore ideas in depth.

I mage of the child as a curious, competent, and caring citizen guides all learning—the program is guided by its fundamental recognition that children are not vulnerable to destructive emotions and in need of training through a system of rewards and punishments, but rather naturally led to develop empathetic relationships from which knowledge and well-being are constructed.

C ommunity is developed from meaningful relationships inside and outside of the school—the program recognizes that children are members of a learning community inside the school and are citizens of the community surrounding the school.

Table 10.1.   Accreditation at a Glance

Organization	What/Who They Accredit	How They Accredit	Length of Accreditation Process and Term	Observations
NAEYC	Center-based providers	10 standards with many individual requirements within standards	Open-ended; good for 5 years	Generally viewed as industry leader
NECPA	Center-based providers	Adaptation of NAEYC standards	1 year; good for 3 years	Does not release exact standards until candidate pays
NAC	Center-based providers	6 areas of emphasis encompassing 91 standards	6 months to 2 years; good for 3 years	Formerly known as NACCP
NAFCC	Family providers	Adaptation of NAEYC standards for family provider context	Open-ended; good for 3 years	Does not release exact standards until candidate pays
CPR	Early childhood educators	13 standards of competency across 6 goals	Open-ended; good for 3 years	Highly regarded by NAEYC
NIEER	No accreditation; focus on large-scale studies	N/A	N/A	Produces annual report titled "The State of Preschool"
REGGIO	No accreditation	Inspire	Evolving	Best Practices

Chapter Eleven

What Other Practical Factors Should I Consider in Choosing the Best Early Childhood Education Program for My Child?

The best things in life aren't things.
—John Ruskin

You have explored all of the various ways to pay for early childhood education, and you have analyzed carefully which pedagogical approach would be best suited to your child. Now what? The truth is that choosing the ideal pre-K program for your child involves many factors beyond cost and pedagogy, including the program's reputation in your community and where your neighbors and friends send their children. Other important considerations include practical and tangible considerations such as the program's schedule of days and hours and convenience as well as more personal and intangible considerations such as the warmth of interactions you observed or felt while at a school. This chapter addresses each of these important factors.

While each one of these ingredients should be considered when making your decision as to where to send your child to pre-K, you as a parent should balance these factors in light of your instincts and "gut feeling" as to what is best for your child and family.

A. THE PROGRAM'S SCHEDULE OF DAYS AND HOURS

The program's schedule of days and hours is often a practical initial consideration when determining where to send your child to school. If you need full-time care due to work or other schedules, looking at full-day programs or shorter programs with the option to extend the day (for care before or after school) is prudent. Conversely, if you have a flexible schedule or if your child has had little daycare or other time outside the home, away from his or her primary caregiver, it may make sense to start with a program that is two or three mornings each week. Determining how the program's schedule of days and hours interacts with a parent's work schedule or the schedule of other siblings is a smart place to start when weeding out programs that may or may not be a good fit for your child or family.

Parents may struggle with the decision as to "how much" pre-K is best for their children. The evidence indicates that half-day pre-K plus half-day kindergarten is better for children than full-day kindergarten alone. We also know that, although any amount of time in pre-K is helpful, at least fifteen hours per week are needed to obtain significant benefits and that those benefits tend to dissipate when children attend pre-K more than thirty hours a week. Accordingly, for most children, the optimal amount of hours per week in a pre-K program is between fifteen to thirty, or three to six hours per day if the child attends every day of the week.

But as is always true, parents know their children best. Some may feel that part-time, half-day pre-K is best for their kids, and some parents, of course, may believe that full-day pre-K is best for their children and their families. Parents who prefer to enroll their children in a half-day pre-K program should do so without fear that their children will not become prepared for full-day kindergarten. While the transition from half-day pre-K to full-day kindergarten is significant, most children will have reached sufficient maturity to make that transition when the proper time comes. There is no need to rush them into a mistaken sense of kindergarten "readiness," and doing so may well be harmful to their development.

1. Part Time

Part-time programs generally meet in the morning or afternoon two to four times each week. These programs allow for a gradual transition to schooling and allow more time for out-of-school activities or unstructured time.

Part-time programs themselves vary in terms of what they may include. Some part-time programs have the ability to add on "extras," such as early care or breakfast or after care or lunch. Other programs have enrichment activities (such as another language, a sport, additional art lessons, etc.) the children can participate in addition to the scheduled pre-K program.

2. Full Time

Full-time programs meet five days a week and generally include the same activities as part-time programs along with an added lunch and rest time and additional activities in the early afternoon.

3. Extended Hours

Most programs do not last a full eight-hour workday, though many full-time programs provide before and after care to meet the needs of working parents. If you are looking at a full-time program, it's important to consider the quality and type of before and after care available and what your child will be doing in this time. Many full-time programs follow the local public school calendar, so researching whether care can be provided during the fall/winter/spring break or whether you will need to make alternate arrangements is helpful to do early on.

4. Year-Round Care

Similarly, many programs follow the local public school schedule and therefore only run the duration of the calendar year. While many working parents use local organizations like the YMCA or other camps, or family members to provide child care in the summer months, it may be more convenient for your family if the program you choose has an on-site option for care over school breaks and during the summer.

B. LOCATION

Whether a program's location is convenient is very important to most parents. Some parents may want a school that is close to home to minimize the commute and to increase the likelihood that other neighborhood children are close by and available for carpools and play dates outside of school. This may be a special consideration for parents whose children attend part-time programs, since if a program is not close to the parent's home the parent may spend much of the time his or her child is in school transporting the child to and from the school.

Other parents may prefer a program that is closer to a parent's workplace so that the commuting time can be spent with the child and the parent can drop into the school more quickly and easily. Still other parents may prioritize a program near a grandparent or a babysitter if drop-off and pick-up duties are to be shared with that other individual.

Some parents in more urban areas may prefer programs that are closer to the downtown area to allow for more field trips and authentic learning outside the classroom. Some other parents may prefer more homelike or rural settings that allow for more frequent outdoor experiences in nature.

Consider how far away the program is and whether it is easily accessible in various weather conditions. It may make sense to determine whether there is convenient parking and appropriate drop-off and pick-up areas. Some schools have a drop-off or pick-up "lane" where children are dropped off or picked up directly in front of the school to a teacher or assistant. While this may be extremely convenient, especially if weather conditions are difficult and/or if there are additional siblings who are dropping off or picking up the student, this does not allow as much time for informal communication or dialogue with the teachers or your child in the school and classroom itself. Consider whether there is sufficient parking on site for programs where you take your child into and out of the classroom each day. If there is not, is additional parking easily accessible and affordable?

C. SCHEDULE

Many programs follow a similar schedule. Many start around 9 a.m. and end the day around noon (or have lunch and rest time as well as additional activities, if it is a full-day program). At the beginning of the day, many programs have some sort of greeting time or morning meeting where the children greet their teachers and each other. During this time, the children may sing songs or do finger plays. The children may be given the opportunity to share a bit about themselves and discuss the routine for the day as well as any special or unusual happenings for that day (if, for example, there is going to be a community meal, a visit from the art teacher, a special snack, a birthday, etc.).

Throughout the day, the children should be given time for small and large group activities, time for free choice among intentionally prepared and offered materials for play, time for movement, read aloud, art, and music. Many programs encourage the children to spend as much time as possible outdoors, especially in mild weather. Consider whether your school has sufficient time and space to allow the children to play and learn outside in different types of weather. Consider how much time children have for choice time—time when they get to explore different activities and areas of the classroom freely—and how teachers interact with children during this time. For example, at some schools, this time is highly unstructured and teachers are more or less passive observers. At other schools, children can choose their activities but are given opportunities to engage with and have their learning extended by their classmates and teachers.

At some point in the middle of the day, children will be offered a snack. Consider whether children will gather and share in this mini mealtime together or whether they may approach snack when they are hungry. Consider also whether they are to bring their own snack, whether families take turns bringing snacks for the whole class, or whether snacks are provided. Consider if there are any restrictions on what foods may be brought into the school—for example, given the recent prevalence of peanut allergies, many schools now strive to be nut-free facilities and therefore any snacks containing peanut butter or the like are prohibited. Consider whether the children have the opportunity to serve themselves their snack and/or the opportunity to clean up the table. Some programs allow children to use real glass cups and ceramic plates or bowls, demonstrating to the children that they are trusted with these fragile things.

At the end of the day, it is typical for the children to gather once more to discuss what they did that day and to sing goodbye songs and say goodbye to their classmates and teachers. At many schools, parents can pick up children and see what the children did that day (painted pumpkins, threaded colored noodles on string, worked on a class mosaic, etc.). Children often excitedly describe with pride the parts of the day that were most memorable to them and spend time happily discussing the day's events with other children and parents. This is often a good time for parents to engage with their child's teachers.

It's incredibly helpful to ask for the early childhood education program's schedule and to see how much the program follows a daily routine. Children—especially very young children—thrive on routine. Accordingly, a program that has a set schedule and routine, that prepares children for transitions, and that takes the time to talk to children about any anticipated breaks from the routine (such as a special visitor, a teacher being out of the classroom, classmates being sick or on vacation, etc.) will be an environment that feels safe and welcoming for a young child.

D. SICK CARE

An important factor to consider especially for families where all parent(s)/caregiver(s) work outside the home is whether the program has a place for your child to go when he or she is sick. Some programs offer a separate, often off-site location for sick children to go to when the child is unable to stay home for any reason. This may be a particularly important factor for your family to consider if it would be very difficult for a caregiver to take off work to stay home with a sick child.

E. TRANSPORTATION

Transportation may be provided to some public programs. In large part, however, most families will be responsible for transporting their own children to school. If other children in the neighborhood attend the same program and there are sufficient car seats in any cars that are used for taking the child to school, carpooling may be an option. If public transportation is available, it may be helpful to take a trial ride on the bus or train to your school to see just how long it takes to get there and back. If you are fortunate enough to have an excellent program within walking distance, this may, of course, weigh heavily in favor of choosing that program for your child.

F. WHERE NEIGHBORHOOD CHILDREN GO TO SCHOOL

Where other children in the neighborhood go to school is another factor to consider. As mentioned above, if children go to the same school, carpooling duties may be shared. Additionally, the ease of collaboration among parents and children may prove beneficial. There is comfort in knowing that other community members are sending their children to a program they have researched and are happy with, and there is an opportunity to further build community within a neighborhood when children share their pre-K experience.

G. GROUPING OF CHILDREN WITHIN THE SCHOOL

Another factor to consider is how children are grouped within the school. In many schools, children are grouped exclusively by age—there is a three-year-old room and a four-year-old room, for example. In other schools, a mixed-age classroom is an option or may even be customary (for example, traditional Montessori classrooms are always mixed age). Families who choose to have their children attend a school where the children are separated based on age may appreciate the additional structure and clarity surrounding the different aspects of each class, and the fact that the children may progress from one year of pre-K to the next on the same schedule and with the same peers. Families who choose to have their children attend mixed-age programs may appreciate the different developmental stages of the children in the same room and the opportunity for the children to build relationships, recognizing their different abilities at different ages and levels.

Families of children who have birthdays close to the cut-off day for kindergarten admittance may also want to pay special attention to whether the program has a "young 5s" program. These programs—which offer a potential third year of pre-K for children who would otherwise be on the younger end of their kindergarten class—have increased in recent years.

The practice of enrolling a child who is otherwise eligible to attend kindergarten for an additional year of preschool so that the child can mature before kindergarten is known as "redshirting." Some parents choose this route hoping that the additional year of social and emotional learning in preschool will help their child to succeed in kindergarten.

In a neighborhood where many choose to redshirt their child, however, it is not uncommon for the kindergarten class to include children with ages spanning over two years. If you are considering redshirting your child, you should be aware that this two-year gap will follow your child into the upper grades. When making this decision, therefore, you should confer with your child's current preschool teachers and administrators and with the local school district.

H. APPROACHES AND PHILOSOPHY

As mentioned above, some programs may tend to use an approach focused on direct instruction while others are more focused on the child constructing his or her own knowledge by himself or herself and/or in conjunction with the teacher. While we have explained in great detail the many benefits of the social constructivist approach—including but not limited to the increased intersubjectivity, executive function, and well-being these programs provide—this is certainly a factor to consider, especially taking into account your own child's needs and personality.

I. LANGUAGE USED: PLAY-BASED VERSUS ACADEMIC

Closely related to the approach and philosophy of the school and, oftentimes, an indication of the school's approach and philosophy is the language the school uses to describe itself. Pay close attention to how the school describes itself on its website and materials as well as how teachers and administrators describe the school. A school that focuses on assessment or making your child "kindergarten ready" may appear to be more academic.

But families should be wary of any program that touts kindergarten "readiness" by suggesting that children will be taught narrowly defined academic skills that can be measured on traditional standardized tests. A website that focuses on helping your child become caring, communicative, and collaborative may use a more play-based and/or social constructivist approach. These practices develop competencies that foster genuine readiness for school, and for life beyond school.

J. CLASS SIZE

Another consideration is class size. Smaller classes may allow for a more intimate, calmer experience as well as, importantly, more teacher attention to each child. Smaller classes do, however, necessarily limit the number of children your child interacts with, thereby providing him or her with fewer playmates and viewpoints to consider. Smaller classes may also make the transition to a kindergarten program with a much larger class more difficult, although the child who has had the opportunity to develop social skills in a smaller group may be better equipped than a child largely overlooked in a larger class to enter a full kindergarten classroom.

Larger classes provide, necessarily, more children for your child to socialize with and, similarly, more families to connect with and build relationships outside of the school.

The NIEER recommends twenty or fewer students for a class of three- or four-year-olds.

K. TEACHER/STUDENT RATIO

Closely related to class size is the teacher/student ratio. The NIEER recommends a ratio of one teacher to ten students or better; in many communities, it is common to have one teacher or staff person for every six to eight children. The more teachers and assistants there are in the classroom, the more they can support each other and the children as well as plan, execute, and document the learning taking place in the classroom.

L. TEACHERS

Teachers should use effective and appropriate strategies that enhance learning and development, recognizing the unique learning styles, needs, and interests of each child in the classroom. Teachers should modify their strategies to respond to these styles, needs, and interests when appropriate. The NIEER recommends that teachers have a bachelor's degree and some specialized training in early childhood education, and that teachers engage in ongoing professional development.

It may be tempting to judge a teacher based on how long he or she has been teaching or how long the teacher has been at a particular school, and, while this may be relevant or telling to some degree, a teacher's warmth and interactions with the children is paramount.

M. SPACE

The space from one program to the next may vary dramatically. Some early childhood education programs are housed in very homelike environments and are self-contained. Others are in small buildings of their own connected by an atrium or lobby of sorts. Still others are classrooms in larger school buildings that may serve students through elementary or middle school or beyond.

Space is—in a Reggio-inspired school—so highly valued that it is referred to as "our third teacher." Ideally, there will be a large central space for children to gather and plentiful natural light. Within the space, materials for children's work and play are easily accessible and displayed in an appealing fashion. Light and mirrors are prevalent. Dress-up clothes, interesting materials, kitchens, photographs, and examples of collaborative children's work are readily available and visible.

N. MATERIALS

Children use materials to express their complex ideas, so materials should be accessible, organized, and authentic. They should be within easy reach of the children. There should be materials out that allow children to collaborate, and the materials presented over the course of a year should progress from more simple to complex.

Materials typically seen in an excellent early childhood environment include unit blocks of various shapes, large hollow blocks, crayons, paint, paper, dishes, dolls, tools, raw materials, and more. The materials should be attractive and include natural items such as leaves, seeds, sticks, shells, and stones and beautiful objects such as ribbon, lace, buttons, and wire.

Sensory tables, such as those that can be filled with water and sand, should be available for small group exploration, as should collaborative work surfaces where children can paint or mold clay together.

Materials exist to facilitate learning relationships and thus can change over time due to the needs of the students. Children should, however, always have daily opportunities to experiment with a variety of materials and tools to express their understandings.

O. INTERACTIONS

The program should promote positive relationships among children and adults, and the interactions, as such, should further these relationships. You should feel welcome from the very first time you or your child visit a program. There should be a plan to help new children with the transition to school so that they can adjust to the program and make friends with other children. Teachers should help children negotiate and resolve conflicts by talking about their feelings and the problems and potential solutions to the problems they encounter.

P. WARMTH

The warmth in the program should be evident. Teachers should engage in warm, friendly conversations with the children and encourage the children to play and work together.

Q. MISCELLANEOUS FACTORS

Other considerations include:

- Does the child have to be potty trained? If not, does the school help with potty training?
- What other supports does the school have available to families? Are there specialists, including mental health experts, available for family consultations?
- In what ways does the school try to create community? Are there community meals or family art nights?
- How welcome are parents in the school? Are parents discouraged or encouraged to visit the classroom?
- Is there a preference given to younger siblings once an older sibling is in school? Is there a tuition break for having more than one student enrolled in school, if the program is private?

Chapter Twelve

How Will I Recognize the Program That's Best for My Child?

Tell me what you pay attention to and I will tell you who you are.
—Jose Ortega y Gasset

No one knows your child better than you. Based on your knowledge of the different ways to pay for pre-K, the variety of pedagogical approaches to early childhood programs, the benefits of social constructivist programs, and other practical factors to be considered, you are now prepared to begin the process of choosing a particular program for your child. In order to make a fully informed choice, you should: (1) engage in research both via the Internet and otherwise to select schools that may be a good fit for your child; (2) visit programs that may be a good fit for your child; and (3) talk with school administrators, teachers, and other parents.

A. WHAT SHOULD I LOOK FOR ON THE PROGRAM'S WEBSITE AND IN ITS PROMOTIONAL MATERIALS?

As a parent, you should first talk to other parents and community members you trust to get a sense of what types of high-quality programs are available where you live. Often, local libraries or other public spaces hold early childhood education fairs where you may have an opportunity to meet with teachers or administrators from various programs. Many communities have groups via social media websites or email listservs where parents can post information about early childhood education programs or ask questions about specific programs.

If you are fortunate to live in an area where there are many options, you should focus your search by engaging in Internet research to analyze each program's website and promotional materials as an informed consumer. These materials often speak in loaded language or code words about a program's approach. In this section, we decode a program's marketing language.

1. Curriculum

When the website talks about curriculum, look for key words that recognize the natural curiosity and amazement children find in learning. The promotional materials should be student centered in that they should recognize that students should be the ones exploring and explaining their thought processes. There should be emphasis on teachers using methods to help the students feel successful and to grow.

a. Literacy

- Does the website or promotional materials mention creating a rich environment? Are books used throughout the day as well as cross-disciplinary activities involving art, math, science, and more?
- Does the website or promotional materials acknowledge that children learn words and oral language activities through circle time, morning meeting, show and tell, snack time, and small group activities with friends?
- Are there areas in the classroom that have open-ended dress-up materials such as colorful scarves, props, kitchens, and more to allow children to dramatize and engage in meaningful play, story acting, and storytelling? Dress-up options should include those not identified with a particular marketed character or gender.
- Emphasis should not be solely on memorizing letters and sounds but rather on creating a literacy-rich environment. Speaking, listening, reading, and writing are connected. The emphasis should be on fostering your child's growing sense of self through comprehending stories and organizing and expressing thoughts and feelings.

b. Math

- Are children given the ability to use math to solve real-life problems?
- Do children get to play and experiment with mathematical concepts and constructs?
- Are there opportunities for children to use math manipulatives, categorize, create patterns, and play with shapes, size, and symmetry?
- Emphasis should not be on memorization of math facts.

- Mathematics should emerge naturally from the interests of the children.

2. Approach

Programs may not always directly state what type of pedagogy or method they use. There are certain words they may use in their materials that indicate whether a program relies more heavily on direct instruction or tends to use more social constructivist methods, however.

a. Direct Instruction

A program that uses direct instruction may state that activities are "teacher led" or may focus on making your child "kindergarten ready." The focus will be on academic skills and prescribed curriculum, specifically memorizing or tracing letters and numbers. There may be a "letter of the week" or worksheets available for students. These programs may also advertise their ability to prepare children to perform well on standardized tests.

b. Constructivist

A program that uses a constructivist philosophy is one that focuses on the independence of the child. The program materials may discuss routine and organization. They also will emphasize teaching children to complete specific tasks on their own, and at their own pace. The program may also advertise the materials that children are directed to work with, including blocks, weights, and balances.

c. Social Constructivist

A program that is social constructivist in nature will be focused on relationships. It will emphasize building relationships between children and among children, parents, teachers, and community members. The "curriculum" in a social constructivist program is "emergent"—it is one that is, in part, driven by children's interests and discoveries.

Rather than mentioning worksheets or mastery of specific academic skills, promotional materials for a social constructivist program will emphasize developing a lifelong love of learning through a child-centered approach based on discovery, guided play, collaboration, negotiation, storytelling, story acting, shared short-term and long-term projects, small and large group work, and many forms of expression.

Social constructivist programs recognize that children are creative, curious, and caring and that a focus on community is essential. Their advertising materials will also emphasize the partnership between you and your child's school. They will encourage you to be an active learner along with your child. And they will make the process and products of your child's learning visible to you through multiple forms of communication with you, including frequent meetings with you, portfolios of your child's work, newsletters, blogs, and shared in-school learning experiences with your child.

B. WHAT SHOULD I LOOK FOR WHEN I VISIT THE PROGRAM?

Now that you've analyzed the program's website and promotional materials, you are ready to schedule visits to those programs that pique your interest. The school visit is an indispensable aspect of any choice regarding early childhood opportunities. This section helps families to recognize in a school environment the particular educational methods and goals used in that school or center.

What should families look for in a school? How do the teachers interact with the children? What materials are available to children? How does the environment support learning? Are children respected and enabled to develop relationships? This section offers a template for capturing critical observations of the school environment.

1. The School

The physical environment is often the first thing a parent notices about a school and should not be overlooked. Schools inspired by the Reggio Emilia approach refer to the school's environment as the "third teacher."

The outside of the school should be welcoming. The best early childhood learning environments display children's work outside the school and in the entranceway to draw parents and caregivers in. They have signs inviting children and families to be a part of the learning that takes place. Some schools may even have signs near the doorway that provide information about what the children have been doing recently and will be doing that day. They even invite families to come in for coffee in the morning.

The school environment, of course, must also be safe and healthy. Ideally, there should be a large outdoor space where children can run, play, and explore the natural world each day.

The classroom should be warm and inviting. Inside the classroom, materials for children's work and play should be easy to reach and carefully arranged to encourage children to explore their interests. The materials available for students to use should be attractive, natural, and beautiful.

The classroom should be structured with small-group learning areas filled with interesting objects and materials such as blocks, reading materials, or sensory tables. Photographs of the children and examples of the children's work should be intentionally displayed. Dress-up materials, kitchens, and attractive materials should be visible. There should be furniture that invites children to collaborate, engage, and discover. The room should be set up to encourage the fluid movement of children from one area to the other.

Ideally, there should be large windows and/or a wide use of mirrors to allow for the appreciation of natural shadows and light. But there should also be sources of shadows and light throughout the environment, such as over-head projectors, prisms, translucent objects, reflectors, and spotlights.

In addition, the environment should include areas for drama, storytelling, and story acting. Does the school have costumes, puppets, and platforms for role-playing?

The environment also should include a rich variety of materials for artis-tic expression. At a minimum, are there easels, paints, and brushes? Does the school have natural materials that are used for individual and group art pro jects, including clay, pine cones, twigs, leaves, acorns, and shells? Are there other repurposed materials such as buttons, string, connectors, wood, and plastic objects that can be used by children to express themselves in many different ways? While many schools have a separate area devoted to artistic expression, the best learning environments are those in which art supplies are integrated into all that the children do.

Where the school or center has multiple classrooms, the doorways be-tween the classrooms should be open, welcoming children to connect with one another. The environment should encourage children to explore other classroom environments and to develop relationships with children who may not be their same age.

2. The Teacher

The most important indication of quality in an early learning environment is the nature of the interactions between teachers and children. The best early childhood education programs are those in which highly trained, skilled, and valued professional educators create a learning environment that encourages children to construct their own knowledge by building meaningful relation-ships.

Accordingly, when you visit a program, try to observe the interactions between the teachers and the children. The quality of those interactions will provide invaluable insight into the quality of the school. The teachers should be actively listening and observing children's learning to make learning vis-ible and to draw out children's interests, feelings, and ideas. As you walk around the room, ask yourself: Are the teachers in this school really listening, observing, reflecting, negotiating, and responding to children and to each other in real time? Are these teachers truly connecting with children? If so, you have found an environment in which your child will achieve great suc-cess and well-being.

Teachers should be flexible. They should recognize that the learning process changes based on children's discoveries. They should use any newly formed or expressed interests to extend learning by creating different, additional activities.

Teachers should recognize that children are capable, creative, curious, caring, and connected members of the community. They should see that children have many strengths and are very capable. While research has shown that direct vague praise ("good job") is not helpful in building children's competencies or self-worth, teachers who acknowledge children's efforts and growth with smiles, eye contact, and words of encouragement are building the kinds of relationships that instill a sense of accomplishment and possibility in children. Teachers' formal training in early childhood development may vary widely. It is wise to determine that each classroom includes at least one teacher with a bachelor's degree in early childhood development/early childhood education.

- Is the program mixed-age or same age? While both types of programs have advantages and disadvantages, seek to determine whether the teachers themselves are confident in their ability to build relationships and support learners at very different stages of development in the existing environment.
- What is the teacher to student ratio and the class size? (These are different!)
- What does the school emphasize? (Art, music, outdoor play, a second language, etc.)

C. WHAT SHOULD I CONSIDER WHEN VISITING WITH ADMINISTRATORS AND TEACHERS?

Families should take the time to visit with school administrators. They should ask the school's educational professionals important questions about the school's philosophy and practices, while maintaining a respectful relationship with those professionals. The following is a list of respectful questions that families may wish to ask during their meeting with school leaders:

1. You have such tremendous experience and expertise. Please share with me your image of a child. Do you see children as capable, curious, and caring citizens who should be encouraged to construct their own knowledge by building meaningful relationships? Or do you believe that children should be shaped by a system of rewards and punishments?

2. I am sure that you understand the qualities that make an outstanding teacher. Do you value a teacher's ability to cover and test particular information, or do you value a teacher's ability to really connect with children, to encourage children to construct their knowledge through meaningful relationships, and to create a caring learning community in and out of the classroom?

3. I am really curious to understand the goal of your program. Is your goal to create a learning community that includes all children? Or, is your objective to find ways to separate children based on your perception of their level of preparation for the next stage of their education?

4. Please help me to understand your view of my role. How do you believe that parents like me should relate to the educators in your school? Do you believe that parents should be welcomed as partners with teachers in my child's learning? Or, do you believe that parents should leave the teachers alone to do their job without parental interference?

5. In light of your experience and expertise, how will you determine whether or not my child is learning? Will you make the process and products of my child's learning visible to me in many ways? Or, will you only give me the results of my child's performance on tests in traditionally tested subjects?

6. From your expert perspective, what is the purpose of education? Is the purpose to encourage children to be collaborative, caring innovators, designers, and leaders in a vibrant democracy? Or do you believe that the purpose of education is to train children to be passive consumers of information and to be able to produce that information in a standardized testing format?

7. Please help me to understand how you perceive the role of racial, ethnic, linguistic, and socioeconomic diversity in your program. Do you understand diversity as something to be tolerated and managed, or do you actively seek and celebrate diversity as a source of great strength in a community of learning?

8. Based on your professional judgment, how should children be disciplined by the teachers or administrators in your program? Will you communicate with my child in a respectful way to determine the root causes of any behavioral concerns and connect with my child and other children to provide developmentally appropriate and classwide strategies for improvement, including restorative justice? Or, will you try to change my child's behavior through punishments such as physical or emotional pain, restraints, timeouts, suspensions, and expulsions?

9. I am really curious to know how your program treats students with special needs. Do you separate them from the group to make sure they

do not upset the learning, or do you try to include them in the class-room community to the greatest extent possible? Do you counsel families who have special needs children that this program may not be a good "fit" for them, or do you welcome them as contributing members of your community?

10. Based upon your experience, what is your approach to children who seem to learn in different ways and at different rates? Do you push all children to achieve in the same way and at the same pace, or do you respond to each child's different learning styles and strengths?

11. You must have encountered families who believe that their children are bored in the classroom or not sufficiently challenged. How do you respond to that kind of concern? Do you cater to parents who believe that their children have an entitlement not to be bored, or an entitlement not to have to put up with other children who do not seem to be achieving at their same rate? Or, do you help families to understand that a child who claims to be bored in a classroom may have room for tremendous improvement in their social and emotional intelligence and in their capacity to develop meaningful relationships?

12. I know that you share my wish that my child achieves great success. Do you define kindergarten readiness as preparing children to perform on standardized tests of traditional academic skills, or do you care more about my child's lifelong success and well-being?

13. I know that resources are tight. What are your priorities in how you spend your scarce resources?

14. Do you believe it's important to attract and retain high-quality teachers and provide them with ongoing professional development opportunities? What is your staff turnover rate?

Part II

How Do I Support My Child by Strengthening Relationships between School and Home?

Part II offers to families, teachers, and administrators (and teachers of teachers and administrators) proven strategies for developing respectful relationships that support learning. This part also helps families and educators achieve coherence between the learning that takes place at home and at school. It shows families how to bring home and to the upper grades the same kind of social constructivist practices that take place in an effective early childhood education program.

Chapter Thirteen

How Can I Partner with Teachers and Administrators to Support My Child's Learning?

Education is that whole system of human training within and without the school house walls.
—W. E. B. Du Bois

This chapter provides effective ways for families to interact with educational professionals at drop off and pick up. It also recognizes that many parents and families simply do not have time to be present at the school during the school day. The book validates those time constraints and suggests creative ways for families to nonetheless be active partners in learning. This chapter also suggests ways in which families can model for their children respect for educational professionals in all of their interactions with the school.

A. CONNECTING AT THE SCHOOL

There are multiple ways to interact with your child's teachers and other educational professionals at the school building itself. In some schools, interaction with teachers is possible when you drop your child off at school and/or when you pick your child up at the end of the day. When staffing permits the teacher to engage with you rather than with the children, this can be a wonderful time not only to learn more about your child and his or her progress but also to learn about your child's teachers themselves.

In some schools, drop off and pick up occur outside of the classroom. At other schools, drop off and pick up take place inside the school or the classroom itself. When you are first visiting schools, inquire about the drop-off and pick-up process. At some schools, where children begin the day outside at a play structure, for example, parents may linger and have a greater opportunity to have informal conversation with both the teachers and other parents, thereby creating and later facilitating a sense of community. At this time, when children are present, it is important to refer to the teacher by the name the children call the teacher—for example, "Mr. Smith" or "Ms. Katie."

Parents should take care to avoid speaking about adult topics, such as troubling personal circumstances or concerns about particular behaviors your child may be exhibiting. Instead, ask the teacher if drop off and pick up are good times to ask open-ended questions about the learning taking place in the classroom and to encourage conversations among parents, teachers, and children.

Be aware that a teacher might suggest a different time to communicate, when she is not helping children transition. At drop off, asking your child simple questions such as "What do you think is going to be in the sensory table this week?" or "What are you most excited to do today?" can help you learn more about your child's experience and help the teacher learn more about what interests your child. If the teacher is available, asking what the children are going to be doing that particular day or what your child has been expressing interest in during choice time demonstrates your desire to deepen the parent/teacher relationship and understand the happenings of the classroom.

Similarly, at pick up, asking open-ended questions such as "What materials did Addie enjoy using today?" and "How did Lakshmi interact with her classmates today?" can be just moments long but can provide great insight into your child's day—and often, very happy anecdotes!

Another way to connect with professionals at your child's school is to spend time within the classroom during the school day. Schools embrace this idea to varying degrees, so it may be helpful to ask what the hopes are for parent involvement within the school day. In schools that use the Reggio Emilia approach, parents are often invited to connect and may be asked to do so in a more structured fashion—by reading stories, talking about special family traditions (for example, if some children celebrate Diwali, parents may be invited to discuss that holiday with the children), bringing in special family foods to eat, or sharing particular skills such as woodworking that will help the children extend ongoing explorations.

B. CONNECTING OUTSIDE THE SCHOOL

Many parents and caregivers are unable to spend significant time within the classroom during the workday. This does not, in any way, diminish your capacity to have a meaningful relationship with your child's teachers. There are other ways to connect with your child's teachers outside the school day.

First, it is always beneficial to ask the teacher how he or she prefers to communicate about your child's daily experience and/or your questions or concerns about your child's school day. As mentioned above, many professionals recommend against having any adult conversations in front of the children and thus may recommend scheduling meetings or communicating via email for any special reason or concern.

To connect on a more regular basis, a question to ask when picking a school and after observing how the professionals interact with parents is how your child's teachers document your child's learning. Many teachers create regular email summaries or share blog posts with families that include descriptions of what the children are doing in the class, conversations the children have had during the school day, and pictures of the students as they engage in various projects at school. Reading these email or blog posts, commenting on the blog posts and emails, and engaging in dialogue with your child's teachers are convenient and efficient ways to connect with the professionals at your school.

C. HOW TO CONNECT

Families can model respect for their children and respect for educational professionals in all of their interactions with the school.

- Refer to professionals by their preferred name.
- Greet the professionals by name when you first see them.
- Inquire into the professionals' lives—how they are doing, what their families are like, what they do over the weekend, what their hobbies and interests are, and more.
- Provide support to the professionals by offering to bring in materials or snacks, or by offering marketing help to the school, attending parent and school meetings, and more.
- Encourage and enable professionals to attend professional development.

You might encourage your school to explore innovative and effective methods of building relationships between school and family. One example would be a school that offers parents the opportunity to participate in a small group of dyads during the school day. A dyad, in this instance, is composed of a parent (or caregiver) and child. A group of three or four dyads meet at a time during the regular school day that is convenient for their schedule. They join together in a particular shared project. Documentation of these sessions is created by a facilitator and shared with families. Families are encouraged to reflect on what they learned about how young children learn. Outlined below are the logistics of establishing these small groups of dyads, examples of how they operate, and demonstrations of their value in building learning relationships.

A second way for a teacher to involve parents in children's learning is to invite parents into the classroom to write down individual children's stories and to help them act them out in small or whole groups. Both dyads and story writing and story acting are outlined in more detail below for parents who wish to introduce these activities to their child's school.

D. PARENT AND CHILD DYADS

In some schools, a studio art teacher, or *atelierista*, works with children, teachers, and families to inspire and support work with beautiful materials in the school's studio and in classrooms. It is possible for this atelierista to work with teachers to offer parents the experience of working in the studio with their child, in a small group including no more than four other families. We refer to these parent/child opportunities as "dyads," and they are opportunities for a parent to work closely with their child and observe the learning process.

These opportunities have been very successful in educating families about how learning is socially constructed, and they help parents understand how learning takes place in the classroom. Even an individual who lacks the formal art training that would make one a true atelierista can act in such a role to offer parents a unique opportunity to engage in small group work with their child and a small number of other parent/child dyads from their child's class.

1. Invitation

To do this, first, there should be an invitation extended to parents that explains this new opportunity. A sample invitation may read:

NEW! Parent/Child Studio Days

Dear Parents;

We know that you are always interested in your child's learning, and it is our goal to make more of this learning visible to you. To make the creative processes we support at school more visible, and to give your child a special opportunity to share his/her "world" with you, we are preparing to host a series of opportunities for you to visit the flexible mini-atelier (studio space) that we have created. Beginning after the first of the year, we will offer you the chance to explore materials in the Gathering Space with your child. We prefer to do this in dyads (e.g., parent/child) and with no more than four dyads at a time. We ask those with twins to schedule time with each individual child. This is an opportunity to have special time with your child around an interesting question, with interesting materials, to observe him or her, and to reflect on what you see, hear, and experience.

The Schedule:

- Begin by creating a collaborative creation with your child (in response to a given provocation/question/problem and in materials that are provided).
- While you are engaged with your child, I will be documenting the learning that is happening.
- Each dyad shares a little about their process with the group.
- The children return to their regularly scheduled classroom activity.
- Parents remain gathered to dialogue with [the facilitator] about the learning small group work supports. We are likely also to speak about the practices at our school and to think about how educational philosophy underlies all of our interactions with children.
- We will observe in your child's classroom, and [the facilitator] will speak about small group work there, and how the process of documentation supports learning.

A suggested link to read before we meet:
Five Reasons to Stop Saying "Good Job," by Alfie Kohn, at http://www.alfiekohn.org/parenting/gj.htm (2001).

Looking forward to sharing this experience. A list of dates/times is attached.

The "Good Job" article is suggested because many adults, wanting to encourage their child, overuse that phrase. Kohn succinctly shows why, rather than offering these words of praise, adults might want to consider stating what we notice about the child's work (e.g., "I see that you have been working for a long time and have chosen different shades of green for your leaves."). He makes a pretty strong case that these two simple words can seem, in some contexts, dismissive and even manipulative, and can lessen a child's internal motivation to express himself or herself. He also suggests that noticing the child's work in a particular way can motivate the child to extend his or her learning and share his or her thinking.

In considering how best to create meaningful relationships with parents, teachers should realize that many parents will have difficulty taking time away from their jobs or other responsibilities to join their children at school. In setting the times, it is important to be careful to accommodate the families' schedules to make sure that as many as possible could participate. Offering multiple opportunities, attempting to schedule families into the available dates on a first-come, first-served basis, and, whenever possible, working with families well in advance to set their dyads (and sometimes triads) on days and times that they could manage proves helpful. While it might not be possible to involve every parent or caregiver in this particular experience, it is important to offer a variety of opportunities.

2. Studio Days

On a child's "studio" day, parents arrive to find the common gathering space arranged as a thoughtful studio space. Tables and chairs are arranged to support dialogue among participants, and materials are carefully chosen and arranged to inspire open-ended creativity of children and adults.

A typed agenda for 1.5 hours together is available, although not emphasized. A sample schedule might include: a fifteen-minute introductory activity while everyone arrives, a thirty-minute activity, fifteen minutes to reflect with the children, about fifteen minutes to reflect with the parents on what they learned from the experience, and about fifteen minutes to visit the classroom (if the teacher and children were available at that time) to observe evidence (documentation and otherwise) of explorations, discoveries, and learning.

In one educational professional's experience with this exact activity, she noted that:

The first three minutes of the session were to me the most enlightening and felt the most risky. Parents and children would approach the table and take seats next to one another. They would look over the array of materials, and then they would anxiously wait for instruction. No two sessions were the same, but a typical session would unfold as follows: I would ask the children if they knew anything about the materials in front of them. Sometimes they would say they look like something they had used before, or they would pick up a watercolor brush or pastel to experiment. A parent would wonder aloud what they should do . . . Should I help my child? The anxiety of each parent's intent to "do the right thing" was palpable. I reflected that most, if not all, of their previous experience at school was in situations where they were told fairly explicitly what their role would be (e.g., sit quietly, engage every child in this activity, give a presentation to the class). I sought to alleviate the anxiety that followed my open-ended invitation to create and to help them to trust themselves. I encouraged them to do whatever came naturally.

All had read the article by Alfie Kohn, and many initially seemed constrained in their dialogue with their child, careful not to use the words *good job*. I continued to make every effort I could to put them at ease. And I would ask the child to explore the materials and "fill their paper with color." The children would then get busy, and the tension around the table would quickly dissipate as the parents felt less responsibility for channeling their child's actions. I walked around, asked open-ended questions, and sometimes stated aloud what I was observing. Parents quickly became engaged with their child and the materials. They also had the chance to observe how others approached the provocation, and how the actions and statements of others (children and adults) in the small group influenced their child.

After a five-minute warning, I would begin to clear the materials off the shared table space and introduce other materials. The materials varied by day, though we always tried to provide manmade and natural materials, repurposed materials, beautiful pieces of ribbon, buttons, lace, and yarn. There were papers of various textures and weights, and instruments for writing. And there were "connectors" such as tape and glue, and less familiar connectors such as wire and string. I shared what an atelierista had once explained to me, that it is important to include connectors because these enable the children to connect their thoughts in concrete ways to create ever more complex ideas.

The next provocation of each session varied, but one session involved asking the children to "make something for someone you love." I encouraged the children to look at the wide range of available materials that we'd selected to speak to the experience and developmental stage of the children. Then I asked the children to talk with their parents and, if they wished, "to make a plan" with paper and pencil before beginning to build their creation. Again, I encouraged the parents to do what came naturally, which resulted in varying degrees and types of engagement with their child, with other children and parents, and with the materials.

After about twenty-five minutes, I gave a five-minute warning and let the children know that they would be returning to the class soon while their parents stayed to talk for a few minutes. The parents and I used the transition time to ask the children to tell us about what they'd made. Throughout the entire session, I documented their actions with photos and words. I strove to capture authentic dialogue. A volunteer parent "documentarian" or teacher able to join the session also documented the learning whenever their schedules permitted.

The children returned to class, and the parents and I were joined, whenever possible, by the child's teacher and by other staff members who know the children well. Some days, teachers who were unable to leave the classroom to participate in the session made sure that they were available to answer parents' questions in the classroom at the end of the session.

We asked questions to encourage reflection: What did you learn about your child? About yourself? About anything? What do you remember about your early learning and kindergarten experience? Was it like this or different? In what ways? What are your hopes for your child's school experience? In the course of our dialogue, parents would invariably note the different times during the session when one child learned from another, one child supported another, one child challenged another to see something from a different perspective. We observed how children would strive to improve their creation as a result of what they were hearing and seeing in the small group. We reflected on the discomfort of beginning with an open-ended provocation rather than a focused assignment, and parents noted that it resulted in less competition among the children and more diversity in the ideas expressed and exchanged.

3. Reflecting on Parent and Child Studio Days through a Lens of Co-Construction

Participating families witness firsthand co-construction in their small group. After each studio session, the educational professional can send each participating family a digital album of photos from the session, so that they can share it with their child and with other family members and reflect on the experience. These pictures and a description as to how children learned through relationships can also be posted on the class blog.

Parent and Child Studio Opportunities are designed to make visible to families, in a carefully planned environment, given ample time and limited transitions, how the relationships that small group interactions make possible support learning. The documentation shared with families through the blog makes visible the learning (by parents, children, and professionals) observed during the sessions.

The small group dynamic encourages ideas to originate with one person and fly around the table. In Eleanor Duckworth's *The Having of Wonderful Ideas: And Other Essays on Teaching and Learning*, she writes that "the development of intelligence is a matter of having wonderful ideas. . . . When children are afforded the occasions to be intellectually creative—by being offered matter to be concerned about intellectually and by having their ideas accepted—then, not only do they learn about the world, but their general intellectual ability is stimulated as a happy side effect." In sessions, ideas may be overheard, observed, and embraced in equal measure by children and adults alike. Some ideas may be rooted in the child's experiences outside of school in his or her community, while others seem to have origins in familiar children's literature. Still other ideas may be inspired by materials available to the child.

E. MEMORABLE MOMENTS FROM AN EARLY CHILDHOOD EDUCATOR'S STUDIO DAYS

The following section memorializes memorable moments from the same educational professional's experience doing studio days.

1. Ideas Flow from Child to Child

During our initial exploration of color (with oil pastels, bleeding tissue paper, watercolor paper, paper straws, tape, and glue/water), the children expanded and shared their "vocabulary" of the possibilities of each medium. For example, they explored the possibilities of drawing lines, scribbles, and solid areas with oil pastels, and they discovered what happened when they added water with a brush, when they drew on a wet area, and when they smeared with their fingers. "Look! It's furry."

After learning how to bend the copper wire to a desired shape, Adrian says, "It's a bridge." He turns to Ava and exclaims, "Look what I can do with wire!" Across the table, having seen how his friend manipulated the wire to make a bridge, Ben uses wire as a structural support in his work with clay.

In another instance, a child notes that "this is an Easter rabbit with a tail . . . like a little puppet . . . it's a flying thing." Ben begins to tell a story with the character he has created: "It's a bunny going on an adventure around the woods."

One lament I'd heard from many adults was that children would paint stylized rainbow after rainbow, seemingly unwilling or unable to express other ideas in paint. Working side by side with liquid watercolors with deep color values, water-soluble oil pastels, watercolor paper, and soft brushes, the children reached beyond painting simple rainbows and experimented with color intensity, contrast, positive and negative space, and, of course, color mixing.

At one moment, Casey observed another child creating a representation of a house, and he declared that he had painted "a house." His concept of "house" appeared broad enough to include abstract as well as concrete and commonly accepted symbolic representations of a house.

Another example of a child learning from observing another's work occurred when Delilah noticed that Kirby had built a three-dimensional table with her clay and wooden sticks, and an upright three-dimensional character, and written a story about them. Delilah then told her mom, "I will stand (my heart) up and work on the other side." Finally, as they had seen Kirby do, Delilah and her mom wrote a story about their creation.

I noted in the blog that I noticed that every child at the table was inspired to experiment with depth and perspective at some point in the session.

A final example that parents witnessed of ideas traveling around a small group occurred during a student's work with clay. One student, Charlie, told us about his creation: "There's a pond where the bear got salmon. The bear doesn't steal the squirrel's food. The bear has more food. This is the squirrel's hole and this is the squirrel (he drew the squirrel and created it out of clay). And these are bear eggs . . . water . . . and a double rainbow. There is buried treasure. The bear goes outside and finds the maps."

Sarah listened to Charlie's story and said, in a very matter-of-fact tone, "Charlie, bears don't lay eggs. They're mammals." Charlie thought about this and did not respond immediately. He seemed to be logging this fact away. After the children returned to class, Charlie's mom explained that he seemed to be combining information in his story that he had gleaned from multiple nature-based books, at least one about birds. The adults talked about how it is possible that, in his story, from his imagination, it is possible that bears DO lay eggs. As adults we reflected on how important it is for children to dream and imagine and not to be constrained by "facts." Charlie's mom also shared that he exhibited horror at the thought of eating the baby eggs. In his mind, they were baby bears, not edible eggs, and he felt appropriate horror at the idea of eating them. Together we reflected on how much we had learned about Charlie's complex learning process by observing his interactions within this small group.

2. Ideas Flow Between Materials and Children

Colored tape inspired many children to create patterns, build symmetrically, measure and estimate. The available beautiful and "repurposed" materials inspired Brady to create a car: "It's a car with boosters." The clay and other natural materials inspired Jade to create a landscape with "sun, grass . . . " Jade began her clay work before I asked her to draw a plan. But her thinking was flexible enough to put the clay down to draw a plan in the middle of her clay work. "This is special . . . this is the treasure . . . the special rocks." Jade indicated that the tall stick is "the special power." She worked with Mom for several minutes to figure out a way to support the stick with clay. She admired her work.

"The rock (she points) is supposed to be huge." It is clear that Jade was suggesting that it was bigger than the grass. In doing so, she showed us her awareness of scale . . . and let me know that the clay rock represents a much bigger rock, but that she had made it to scale. In the blog, I reflected on Jade's use of symbols. While her clay depicted a very concrete scene (sun, grass, king), she used a stick to symbolize the king's power. And she handily formed letters out of clay, possibly for the first time. I noted in the blog that this shows me that she understands more about how letters are formed than merely how to write them in two dimensions with a writing instrument. She is able to see them and reproduce them in three dimensions.

Finally, Caley was inspired by the pastels and the pattern on her dress to create a similar geometrical pattern. I overheard Caley saying to her dad, "This is going to be very hard." He smiled and whispered something softly to her, and she continued. She started drawing and realized that what she drew "looks like my dress."

She actively referenced the colors and shapes of her dress. She experimented with layers of color and mixed media. "Look what I did! Tissue and then I colored on top!" She recognized that the tissue left a colored print behind. She admired the tissue as if thanking it for the color it left behind. She recognized that she captured a geometric likeness of the pattern in her dress and shared her excitement with her dad.

3. Ideas Flow from Adult to Child

We saw many examples of parents sharing technique with their child. Zane's mom noted that "when you quietly said to Ellie this morning 'I notice that when you overlap the watercolor colors (pink and blue), you create a new color (purple),' her son, sitting across the table from Ellie, heard and began to experiment overlapping strokes with the paintbrush." This mom shared that she could tell that he was listening to me, that he looked at what Ellie had done, and that he began his own independent explorations as a result. He did not copy, but incorporated what he had seen and heard into his existing body of knowledge. This is how children learn and, in fact, how we learn at any age.

Another one of my favorite "aha" moments during the parent/child sessions was when I noticed that a dad wove rich vocabulary into his observations and questions, and that the child used these words with ease when communicating with those in the group. Brian's space station featured an antenna and solar panels, and was not only "eco-friendly" but also "self-sustaining." I noted this as an example of what researchers Betty Hart and Todd R. Risley concluded in their famous study *Meaningful Differences in the Everyday Experience of Young American Children*. Hart and Risley found that while children from different backgrounds typically develop language skills around the same age, the subsequent rate of vocabulary growth is strongly influenced by how much parents talk to their children. These researchers also found that children's academic success at ages nine and ten is attributable to the amount of talk they hear from birth to age three.

4. Ideas Flow from Adult to Child to Adult and On and On

Nina was asked to draw a plan for her clay. Her plan had three drawings of her pot in various stages of creation, from the top to the bottom of the paper. When finished with her pot, she adjusted her plan to become "instructions" for others. Her instructions incorporated and made visible her skills in drawing, sequencing, spacing, numeracy, and literacy.

In another instance, asked to fill her paper with color, Martha picked up a pastel. I overheard her say, "I don't really have a plan. I'm putting the stuff where I want it to go." A bit later in the process, I heard her say, "I really DO have a plan." I asked her about this change of mind, and she thought for a while. She responded with something about "Putting things where I want them to be . . . that's my plan." A short time later she said, "Sometimes when someone says something I like to repeat it over and over in my brain." I asked, "I wonder why you do that?" She responded with a question: "To remember?" This was a sharp reminder to me of how deeply young children are capable of thinking, and particularly of their capacity for metacognition, or thinking about how they learn.

In a dialogue following a session, a parent observed, "It is difficult to resist the impulse to be directive. When open, there are things to surprise. (My son) said 'it's a yoyo someone dropped at the bottom of the ocean.' I wouldn't have heard that if I'd been directive." Another said, "You don't know where they're going to go. You could give her the same materials at another time and she would go somewhere else with them." And another noticed that "what materials you offer first matters. And how you present them matters."

In the same dialogue, we talked about how it happened that one of the class's favorite books, *The Curious Garden* by Peter Brown, led to a classroom project of creating gardens out of geometrically folded paper flowers. The children's appreciation for the story and the illustrations reminded the teacher of her experience visiting the High Line in New York (a park on a former elevated rail line). The assistant teacher in that classroom brought with her a graphic arts background and was able to guide the children in the steps necessary to create three-dimensional flowers of watercolored paper of the children's own design. This class integrated literacy, geometry, and watercolor exploration into an exploration of gardens. The teacher was present for this dialogue, and shared with the parents that she has learned that it is most important to know when to say nothing, to simply wait for a child to offer what he or she is thinking. Her willingness to say nothing is often rewarded with something she could never have expected that child to say, providing new insight into that child's development.

5. Ideas Flow from Adult to Adult

By encouraging families to participate in dialogue after the children returned to class, and to read and comment on the blog afterward, we hoped to expose families to the complexity of the learning process. Parent comments suggested that it became clear to many that no child was an empty vessel, but that each and every child brought interesting knowledge and experiences to the table. This allowed the parents to understand the importance of the learning flowing throughout the community, and to not focus solely on their child's individual learning.

The families' engagement in co-construction also made it clear to many that the most fascinating learning observed was not a result of an adult sharing information with a child but of a child understanding something in a new way because of a new shared experience. Perhaps the most memorable example of this happened on a day when I approached Zane, who had been working in watercolor and pastel.

I crouched to his level at the table and said, "I wonder if you could tell me about what you are doing." From a distance, I had heard Zane and his mom having an extended dialogue about this creation, and I was hoping he would share some of this with me. I gave him lengthy "wait time," but Zane did not offer any information. He looked at his mom, and rather than answering for him she encouraged him to share what they had been talking about. Zane tipped his head slightly (that look that children get when they have an idea) and picked up a pastel.

He began to write letters and words that explained what he'd created. "A.T.A.T." Mom explained to me that this was "Star Wars language," and prompted him to explain it to someone unfamiliar with this language.

He wrote "STAR WARS" to help me understand the vehicle he had made. In his "aha!" moment before he picked up the pastel, Zane seemed to realize that he could express himself not only visually by drawing but also with this shared symbolic language of written letters that he had learned to form and the words he had learned to sound out and spell. In her "aha!" moment, his mom understood that Zane had recognized how meaningful writing and reading could be in expressing and sharing his ideas.

F. REFLECTING ON PARENT AND CHILD STUDIO DAYS THROUGH OTHER LENSES

Using a blog to document studio sessions can emphasize the importance of children, families, and professionals working together over time in a carefully planned environment. Parent comments during the sessions and in survey responses afterward can suggest that parents develop a keener understanding of the importance of small group work in building the kind of community that fosters learning.

There are, however, as many ways in which to interpret or make meaning from admittedly subjective observations as there are readers of a blog. In fact, photos and observations invite readers to see the learning they find visible through the lens of their choice. There are at least three alternative ways through which to view the learning that results from the experience of co-construction: (1) through the lens of dispositions or habits of mind (e.g., collaboration, persistence, negotiation); (2) through the lens of domains (e.g., social, emotional, cognitive, fine and gross motor); and (3) through the lens of subject disciplines (e.g., language arts, mathematics, science, social studies, art). Each of these ways of looking at what transpires during sessions makes visible learning that is important to families who care deeply about their child's education. Parent comments will suggest that they reflect through these alternative lenses on their own child's learning and on the learning of all Studio Day participants.

1. Viewing Documentation through a Lens of Habits of Mind

Lillian Katz has offered the following definition of dispositions, or habits of mind. She notes that dispositions "can be thought of as habits of the mind, tendencies to respond to situations in certain ways. . . . Another requirement for learning particular dispositions is to have the opportunity to behave that way, so that the behavior can be acknowledged and responded to. By acknowledging and appreciating a disposition, you strengthen it."

Others have called these dispositions "executive function skills," or strategies that we all need when confronted with a problem, the resolution of which is not immediately apparent. Executive function skills include the ability to persist, to think flexibly, to gather data through the senses, to create, to imagine, to listen with empathy and understanding, to innovate, to negotiate, to reflect, to apply past knowledge, to express your thoughts clearly, to wonder, to take responsible risks, to find humor, to think independently, and to remain open to continuous learning. As mentioned above, studies in the field of neuroscience involving mirror neurons suggest that young children need to interact with those who model these skills. And studies in psychology show us that these are skills best developed in small groups where children feel emotionally and physically comfortable expressing themselves and experiencing competency.

When we observe closely, we see Adrian's flexible thinking and ability to wonder in his pastel drawing where "fire is meeting with water, dirt is meeting with a rainbow." We see Ava, gathering data from her observations of Adrian, understanding that she, too, can use the brush to spread color. We see Caley's persistence in capturing the pattern of her dress on paper. And when he picked up a pastel to communicate in written words what he chose not to say aloud, Zane showed us his ability to apply past knowledge and to express himself clearly. And Kirby and Delilah showed us their willingness to take responsible risk and create clay objects that can be viewed from multiple perspectives (from above and from each side). In sum, there is much in the documentation shared with parents for them to discern the development of important habits of mind throughout the learning community.

2. Viewing Documentation through a Lens of Domains

Another way to reflect on the learning made visible in a blog's documentation is to view it through a lens of learning domains: social, emotional, cognitive, and fine and gross motor. When Sarah said to Charlie in a very matter-of-fact tone "Charlie, bears don't lay eggs. They're mammals," and Charlie reacted by thinking quietly about what she said, we see the kind of thoughtful dialogue that is certainly nurtured in the children's classroom. We see the consequence of families and teachers modeling how to treat one another with respect. We also see how children develop an ever-changing body of factual cognitive knowledge by sharing their different experiences and knowledge with one another. Again, there is much in the documentation shared with parents for them to see growth in each individual learning domain.

3. Viewing Documentation through a Lens of Subject Disciplines

Yet one more way to view learning made visible is through the lens of subject disciplines. Of course, skills in the visual arts are made visible throughout. Also, language arts skills are evident in Zane's Star Wars creation, in Nina's sequential instructions for making a clay pot, and in Brian's extensive vocabulary. Mathematical skills of estimation, measurement, counting, and patterning are evident in multiple children's exploration with colored tape and in Caley's determination to create a likeness of her dress's fabric. Kirby and Delilah's work required them to balance their clay pieces. Brady's car required the symmetry of parts. Scientific method involving trial and error was at work as Evan experimented with ways to create a long linear object from shorter ones. And documentation made it easy to see Charlie's understanding of what mammals have in common expanding before our eyes!

Excellent early childhood educators emphasize throughout the year the importance of building and strengthening a strong learning community, yet they also understand that each family looks at the documentation teachers provide with unique eyes. Some seek evidence of learning habits of mind, others look for social/emotional development, and still others (or the same families at different times) focus on signs of cognitive learning within traditional subject areas such as language arts, math, and science. Documentation of a shared learning experience is valuable in making visible the learning through whichever lenses are important to a particular family. This is not a coincidence, but evidence of what every experienced early childhood educator knows: that learning in these early years is always crossing domains and disciplines, and that it always involves multiple habits of mind. Especially in the early years, curriculum is not something that can be easily codified but includes all of life that the child experiences. That is why it is so important for families and teaching professionals to communicate effectively through various forms of documentation and to work together to provide each child a set of coherent and meaningful experiences, at school, at home, and in the community.

4. A Second Way to Build Relationships between Home and School

Children learn through sharing stories in meaningful ways. In *The High-Performing Preschool: Story Acting in Head Start Classrooms*, Gillian McNamee sets out a method by which an adult observes in the classroom, asks a child if she has a story to share, writes down that child's story, and offers the child the opportunity to act out the story with peers in a small or whole group. In the course of this activity, the adult has the opportunity to hear the child's story and to observe how the children share their ideas with one another in the course of acting out one child's story. Literacy skills are developed, as are social and emotional skills involved in any collaboration. A parent willing to learn this method of working with children and teachers in the classroom has a front row seat to the way learning happens in the classroom.

Chapter Fourteen

What Is the Best Way to Know If My Child Is Learning?

Stand aside for a while and leave room for learning, observe carefully what children do, and then, if you have understood well, perhaps teaching will be different from before.
—Loris Malaguzzi

Documentation is the process of making visible to multiple stakeholders through multiple media the process and products of individual and group learning. Families who truly aspire to be partners in their children's education must become conversant with documentation. This chapter offers the definitive guide to families and educators about the methods of effective documentation. It also shows how documentation can further enhance the relationships between families and school, and deepen learning.

Guided by what researchers have learned by observing educators engaged in creating documentation and using it in their work with young children, families, and community, this chapter offers strategies for developing the process of documentation, for practicing documentation to deepen learning, and for using documentation as an authentic method of assessing learning and making it visible to multiple stakeholders.

A. THE PROCESS OF DOCUMENTATION

1. Observing

Documentation requires observation of individual and group learning. But observation assumes the involvement of all senses. In particular, the documenter—whether it is a teacher or a family member—must engage in active

127

listening. In "The Pedagogy of Listening," Carla Rinaldi explains how listening can be the basis of any learning relationship:

- Listening should be sensitive to the patterns that connect us to others. Our understanding and our own being are a small part of a broader, integrated knowledge that holds the universe together.
- Listening should be open and sensitive to the need to listen and be listened to and the need to listen with all our senses, not just with our ears.
- Listening should recognize the many languages, symbols, and codes that people use to express themselves and communicate.
- Listening to ourselves—"internal listening"—encourages us to listen to others but, in turn, is generated when others listen to us.
- Listening takes time. When you really listen, you get into the time of dialogue and interior reflection, an interior time that is made up of the present but also past and future time and is therefore outside chronological time. It is a time full of silences.
- Listening is generated by curiosity, desire, doubt, and uncertainty. This is not insecurity but the reassurance that every "truth" is so only if we are aware of its limits and its possible falsification.
- Listening produces questions, not answers.
- Listening is emotion. It is generated by emotions, it is influenced by the emotions of others, and it stimulates emotions.
- Listening should welcome and be open to differences, recognizing the value of others' interpretations and points of view.
- Listening is an active verb, which involves giving an interpretation, giving meaning to the message, and valuing those who are listened to by others.
- Listening is not easy. It requires a deep awareness and a suspension of our judgments and prejudices. It requires openness to change. It demands that we value the unknown and overcome the feeling of emptiness and precariousness that we experience when our certainties are questioned.
- Listening removes the individual from anonymity (and children cannot bear to be anonymous). It legitimizes us and gives us visibility. It enriches both those who listen and those who produce the message.
- Listening is the basis for any learning relationship. Through action and reflection, learning takes shape in the mind of the subject and, through representation and exchange, becomes knowledge and skill.
- Listening takes place within a "listening context," where one learns to listen and narrate, and each individual feels legitimized to represent and offer interpretations of her or his theories through action, emotion, expression, and representation, using symbols and images (the "hundred languages"). Understanding and awareness are generated through sharing and dialogue.

Rinaldi concludes "Thus, the pedagogy of listening is not only a pedagogy for school but also an attitude for life. It can be a tool, but it can also be something more. It means taking responsibility for what we are sharing. If we need to be listened to then listening is one of the most important attitudes for the identity of the human being, starting from the moment of birth."

2. Recording

Documentation involves recording learning in a variety of media, including note taking, texting, audio recording, photographs, video, and blogging. Effective communication of children's learning requires the observer to consider which media will best convey the learning that he or she wishes to convey. Sometimes a child's words are most important, while at other times a child's drawings of their thoughts or theories most accurately reflect their learning. Sometimes, a photo of the child's expression as he or she is engaged in discovery tells more than words or drawings could convey. Other times, the process is best captured in audio or video, so as to convey the thinking process over time.

3. Interpreting

All documentation is subjective. The listener has a unique perspective. Therefore, documentation is made stronger when it brings together a variety of interpretations. Within a school, educators pool their reflections and share their perspectives on a learning experience. This sharing not only strengthens the documentation but also serves as real-time professional development for educators. The educators' shared reflections invariably cause them to think more deeply about their teaching and to try new approaches within the classroom. The very act of documenting with others is a learning relationship that benefits most everyone with a stake in a classroom.

4. Sharing

Documentation envisions sharing the records and interpretations of learning with families beyond the classroom. Once the learning is effectively captured, it needs to be shared. This sharing takes place in many ways:

- Through visually interesting *panels* of photos of children's work displayed in common gathering spaces
- In *individual student portfolios* that highlight learning moments or explorations that involve a particular child or a group that that child was a member of

- In *classroom portfolios* that focus on a particular small or whole group project that emerged and evolved over time within the learning community
- In *newsletters, emails, phone calls, and conferences* between educators and families
- In brief descriptions of the day's explorations (dictated by the children) written and displayed for families who may pick up their children without entering the school
- Through *interactive blogs* that communicate to families small and whole group projects that emerge and evolve over time

As described in chapter 13, one particularly effective way to share documentation and to make learning visible is to invite families into the school to engage with a small group of children and materials around a provocation (e.g., "How do we make lemonade?" Or "I wonder if you could use these materials to make something for someone you love?"), to document the dialogue and the learning that the educator sees happening in this group, and then to share the documentation with families. Adults involved in the activity see firsthand how capturing the dialogue and photos of the children's learning process and reflection results in a deeper understanding of and appreciation for the learning.

They realize, for example, that they did not simply make lemonade with children. Perhaps through dialogue they inspired the children to think about how and where lemons are grown, how they resemble other citrus fruits and how they are different, how fruit is cut safely, how many lemons are needed, and how two halves make a whole. In short, parents involved in such documented learning activities see the literacy, math, and science skills integrated in small group work and begin to see these skills embedded in wider play. Experience has shown that families who begin to think this way create documentation and share with teachers learning observed at home.

All evidence of learning is not equal. Test scores and grades do not necessarily make visible either the depth or breadth of an individual's or a group's learning experience. The learning that takes place in the educational environment must also be made visible to multiple stakeholders. The cornerstone of visible learning is the practice of documentation. As defined by Project Zero and Reggio Children, documentation is the "practice of observing, recording, interpreting and sharing through a variety of media the process and products of learning."

Documentation is essential to the learning process as it is a deliberate act of reflecting on the process of individual and group growth. The documentation informs all subsequent teaching in and outside the classroom. Even more, documentation provides an authentic assessment of the learning process by giving direct evidence of learning that can be shared with the community surrounding the school.

As Lella Gandini, Reggio children liaison in the United States for Dissemination of the Reggio Emilia Approach, has explained, the practice of documentation involves:

- Observing
- Leaving and recording traces of observations
- Interpreting the traces
- Making hypotheses
- Making choices
- Preparing materials and the environment
- Preparing the documentation to share with others
- Revisiting among teachers
- Revisiting with children
- Revisiting with parents

According to Gandini, therefore, documentation begins with skillful observation: "In order to document, one must engage in observation: (1) seeing children and listening to them in an active way; (2) becoming aware of one's own way of interacting with children; and (3) sharing points of view with other educators." But as Gandini also emphasizes, it is "necessary to leave traces of the observations to examine them. There are many ways of leaving traces, which are documents that should be interpreted to understand children better, to share with colleagues, and to know what to do next."

Although documentation may take many different forms, researchers have observed that the practice of documentation by experienced educators includes five common qualities:

- Documentation involves a *specific question* that guides the process.
- Documentation involves collectively *analyzing, interpreting, and evaluating* individual and group observations; it is strengthened by multiple perspectives.
- Documentation *makes use of multiple languages* (different ways of representing and expressing thinking in various media and symbol systems).
- Documentation *makes learning visible* when shared with learners (including children, parents, and teachers).
- Documentation is not only summary. It is *prospective*, as it shapes the design of future contexts for learning.

Documentation makes learning visible for teachers, parents, and children. By documenting, teachers are able to see children better, follow their thinking, and understand their learning. They are able to make predictions, and to enter into action with the children in ways that can be flexibly adjusted according to observations. In taking documentation, teachers become present in the learning process and are better able to reflect on their practice.

Documentation offers parents a window into how their child thinks and learns. It also provides opportunities for parents to know how their child interacts with materials in the environment. It encourages parents to reflect on their child's ability to form meaningful relationships with others. In short, documentation provides parents opportunities to see their child and other children with "new eyes" or in ways they may not ever have noticed before.

Perhaps most important, documentation supports children. It offers them opportunities to revisit, explore further, and to become aware of their own learning. It enables children to engage in metacognition, to assess how they learn so that they may replicate their own successful learning strategies. Documentation also gives children the opportunity to see that their learning is respected and valued.

One teacher captured a photo of a child holding her work and a dialogue that included that child's words about her work making "a ticket for our *Frozen* play." In that case, documentation included both photo and dialogue and enabled multiple audiences to see clearly how a four-year-old (enamored with the Disney musical film *Frozen*) built visual memories from her experience seeing *Frozen and* reading *Frozen* books with family, teachers, and peers. She built motor memories from her experience drawing symbols to represent her ideas. The picture of what she made—three letters from the word *frozen*—shares with the audience the exact moment that those experiences inform her emerging literacy skills—both storytelling and writing. Neither her words nor her drawing independently make her emerging literacy skills visible as powerfully as the two together. And sharing both with the child and her family allows for shared reflection on the child's growth. The teacher also captured the child's response to the question "How did you know how to write *Frozen*?" "I reached back, behind my eyes, and I saw it." It is difficult to imagine more powerful evidence of that child's developing ability to think about her own thinking.

B. PRACTICING DOCUMENTATION TO DEEPEN LEARNING

In the *Relationship between Documentation and Assessment*, Brenda Fyfe describes how documentation can be used to support learning. It provides formative assessment, with *formative* meaning that it is usually carried out throughout an educational experience. Fyfe emphasizes that documentation is meant to support "the learner to participate in looking at his or her own learning to construct or reconstruct new and deeper understandings." Quoting Rinaldi, Fyfe says "It is done to make learning visible so that the learners can 'observe themselves from an external viewpoint while they are learning.'"

When children look at documentation of their work on the wall or in their individual student portfolios, they are prompted to develop the skill of self-reflection. They learn to think about thinking, and their metacognitive skills are strengthened. Their executive functioning skills also are strengthened as they make plans for the future ("I want to do that again . . . only this time, I'll do it differently."). And the documentation guides them in their search for meaning (Why did we cut open that pumpkin? What did we learn? Do all round fruits have seeds inside? How can I know that?).

In addition, documentation can make visible where children are within their individual zones of proximal development. The zone of proximal development is an authentic assessment tool. It enables educators to determine how close the child is to developing particular mental processes.

The assessment cannot be limited to testing the child's ability to do a task independently. Rather, the teacher must first assess the child's behaviors when the teacher or the child's peers are assisting the child. The assessment is designed to determine if the child can engage in a mental process in collaboration with others. If so, then the child and the teacher are within the "zone of proximal development." The teacher can then structure the child's environment to encourage the child to internalize the mental process, and to exercise that process independently.

This method of authentic assessment puts the teacher in the role of a researcher. The teacher provides different forms of assistance to the child to determine which ones enable the child to acquire a particular mental tool. In so doing, the teacher analyzes the mental process by which the particular child constructs knowledge. Once the teacher has discovered with the child the way that child learns, the teacher can then provide effective methods of assistance to the child. These methods of assistance will strengthen the tools the child needs to construct knowledge independently.

A truly effective "curriculum" must emerge from the child, in relation to teachers and peers. Only after the teacher acquires an understanding of how the child thinks in collaboration with others, and how the child proceeds toward independent thinking, can the teacher design effective instructional practices. The fundamental purpose of curriculum is to encourage a child to form meaningful relationships with teachers and peers, which will allow the teacher and the child together to create strategies that will enable the child to internalize higher mental functions. Curriculum therefore must emerge from the children.

The true nature of child development also demonstrates the ineffectiveness of static assessments of a child's performance on a standardized test. Authentic assessments produce insight into the way in which the child's mind works, the way in which the child constructs knowledge. That assessment is necessarily "dynamic." It analyzes how a child processes the various types of assistance provided by more knowledgeable peers and teachers. Some forms of assistance are more effective than others in helping a child to internalize particular higher mental functions. In addition, some collaborative settings may be more helpful to the child than others. Authentic assessment, therefore, must be designed to document the process by which children construct knowledge in collaboration with others.

Documentation also models for children listening, research, and literacy skills. When children observe their teachers documenting learning, they also wish to document their own learning and that of their peers. By modeling the various methods of communicating knowledge, educators inspire children to develop profound literacy skills. As the documentation of a child's own process of learning to write *Frozen* indicates, children who are participants with others in the art of documentation can begin to reflect upon their own ways of learning.

C. USING DOCUMENTATION TO MAKE LEARNING VISIBLE TO MULTIPLE STAKEHOLDERS

Documentation is an authentic assessment of learning. Beyond providing a tool for deepening learning within a classroom, documentation can also make learning visible to important stakeholders outside of the classroom, including:

- Teachers throughout the school
- School administrators
- Taxpayers and other funding sources
- Community members and potential community members
- Policymakers

As Project Zero has recognized, documentation has the potential to replace, or at least augment, traditional inauthentic forms of assessment through standardized testing. Those researchers also suggest that documentation can be used to mediate the "unprecedented focus on high-stakes testing and accountability." They show that "standards" can be woven into the group learning environment. For example, a teacher who reflects on children's learning using terminology found in the Common Core Standards can create a shared vocabulary that reinforces the validity of documentation as an authentic assessment of the full range and depth of student and community learning. By preserving memories and creating history, documentation makes visible the culture of a school. It also can become an effective advocacy tool for educational opportunities for all children. As Lella Gandini has recognized, documentation "sends powerful messages about the richness and potential of children and childhood."

Finally, as Carlina Rinaldi has insightfully stated, documentation of the process and products of individual and community learning develops habits of mind and heart that are vital to the flourishing of a democracy.

Documentation can offer children and adults alike real moments of democracy. Eli's mom, familiar with the teacher's documentation of learning in the classroom, shared with his teachers something he'd written at home. After asking his mom to model how to write the words he wished to write, he wrote, "I love Eli. I love Mom. I love my classmates." On a second page he wrote, "I love my teachers." By documenting his reflections on his identity and his relationships with his family, teachers, and his peers, Eli (age four) made visible his construction of knowledge and meaning through those relationships. What was also documented in myriad ways throughout the year was the goal shared between school and family to strengthen Eli's finger muscles so that he could improve his grip on the writing instrument. The many opportunities he had to write symbols in meaningful contexts within the classroom and at home were fully documented as well. Underlying his ability to focus on his message was the documented healthy separation from his family, and his attachment to educators and peers at school.

Eli recognized the power of his ideas and his ability to share them with those who listen, those he loves. By constructing knowledge through meaningful relationships in a supportive learning community, Eli and his peers become empowered to make their own meaning. The skills of collaboration and self-governance that children develop through learning relationships are vital not only to their individual success and well-being but also to the health of the American democracy. Moreover, through these same relationships, children learn to love learning.

Documentation also recorded Eli joining his friends in the classroom one morning soon after he had shared his feelings about his classmates and teachers. With wonder in his eyes and a smile that enveloped his world, he shared with his teacher: "Every day you get something new in your brain when you go to school. I'm going to get something new in my brain today."

Chapter Fifteen

How Can I Extend My Child's Learning at Home?

There are only two lasting bequests we can hope to give our children. One of these is roots, the other, wings.
—Johann Wolfgang von Goethe

A. CREATING COHERENCE BETWEEN THE CLASSROOM AND THE HOME

Striving to implement social constructivist practices outside of school will create coherence between your home and the classroom. Many of the ingredients of a social constructivist may come very naturally in your home. Others may feel as if they may take more effort to implement.

1. Prioritize Relationships

Spend time with your children one on one. Get down on their level when you speak with them. Make eye contact when you speak to them and truly listen to what they have to say. Ask open-ended questions.

2. Model Collaboration

When there is inevitably a conflict or a problem in your home, work thorough that problem together.

3. Support the Multiple Languages of Your Child

As you well know, your child is unique in how he or she learns and how he or she expresses himself or herself. Encourage self-expression in multiple languages.

4. Give Your Child Time to Explore

Don't overschedule your child. Make time for unstructured play. Spend lots of time outdoors. Go on nature walks and collect beautiful things from nature—vibrantly colored leaves, shiny acorns, or uniquely shaped twigs. Watch bugs crawl. Look for shapes in the clouds. Tell stories about the cloud shapes.

5. Give Your Child Time to Create

Let your child make a mess. Let your child use multiple materials at home—paints, crayons, clay, and playdough. Let your child use sensory materials—play with dry beans, pasta, sand, and stones. Put whipped cream on a cookie sheet and let your child draw.

6. Do Not Be Distracted by Unreliable Short-Term Measures of Academic Performance

In this era dominated by standardized testing, it is very tempting for parents to measure their child's development and an early childhood program's quality by a test score. Parents should resist that temptation. The problems associated with standardized tests are legion. Among those many problems is the fact that standardized test scores do not provide any reliable measure of a student's actual learning, potential for future academic achievement, or long-term success and well-being. Nor do they provide any indication of the quality of the teachers or the learning process.

7. Develop Habits of Mindfulness

Mindfulness is being fully present with your child. That is much easier said than done. Families are incredibly busy with work and other obligations. Screens are a constant source of distraction. Adults often think they are able to effectively multitask. Unfortunately, the research suggests otherwise. Children know when you are not really listening. As difficult as it is to be fully attentive to a child, there are strategies that may be helpful. For example, parents and caregivers may wish to:

• Slow down

- Really listen
- Reserve judgment
- Find time for small moments in each day to make a connection with your child
- Sustain attention to your body, breath, or sensations that arise in each moment
- Make the choice to pay full attention to tone and texture of your child's voice, emotional state, facial gestures, and body language
- Integrate tools such as a mindfulness jar (a jar filled with glycerin and glitter) or singing bowl (a type of bell) into everyday activities. You can draw a parallel between the chaos of the glitter when the jar is shaken and a child's upset. Watching the glitter settle together while breathing deeply often calms both children and adults. Listening to the chime of a singing bowl attentively until the sound is no longer heard can also help bring calm and focus to those listening.

B. A SOCIAL CONSTRUCTIVIST TOOL KIT OF SHARED PRACTICES

Family members can encourage their children to extend and deepen their learning by practicing social constructivist strategies at home. At their core, these strategies include inspiring children to learn with others in shared activities and to make that learning visible.

Families may wish to try these approaches:

- Because learning is about exploring issues rather than digesting information, families should ask children questions rather than provide easy answers.
- Because learning is about embracing nuance and subtlety, families should learn with their children how to untie perplexing cognitive knots.
- Because learning is about struggle, families should support their children in working through tough questions.
- Because learning is about group work, families should encourage their children to come up with answers or solutions together, with friends, siblings, cousins, and caregivers.
- Because learning is about expression, families should partner with their children to make the learning process visible through documentation.
- Because learning is about self-assessment and internal motivation, families should give voice to a child's own assessments of the process and products of his or her learning.

Families can encourage genuine learning in their children by inspiring them to pursue and to share their natural curiosities. The following kinds of phrases may prompt the kind of family interactions that lead to profound growth:

- I wonder?
- What do you think?
- Help me understand . . .
- How did you decide?
- How did you make that?
- I see that you . . .
- I think I hear you saying . . .
- I wonder if you could explain . . .
- I wonder if you could teach me . . .
- How can we solve this together?
- Who might help us?
- How can we share this?
- How does this make you feel?
- I wonder what else you would like to explore?
- I wonder if we could ask someone else?
- How can we draw this?
- How can we remember this?
- I wonder where we could go to explore this some more?
- I wonder how what you learned could help others?
- I wonder what you remember learning?

These moments of shared inquiry not only encourage children to extend and sustain their learning, they also bring great joy to families and lead to lifelong learning.

In 1995, researchers Betty Hart and Todd Risley discovered that children who heard more words by age three were better prepared for school and had bigger vocabularies, were better readers, and received higher test scores by third grade. Hart and Risley had followed pre-K students and tried to improve their vocabulary in an effort to close the achievement gap. They went into the homes of these children every month until they were age three to see what the language-learning environment looked like and found that, by the end of age three, children born into poverty will have heard thirty million less words than their more affluent peers. They also found that not only did these children born into poverty hear fewer words, they heard less-complex words.

Dana Suskind, the director of the Thirty Million Words Initiative, author of *Thirty Million Words: Building a Child's Brain*, and scientist, surgeon, and social activist at the University of Chicago, has dedicated her life's work to addressing this deficit. She has identified what she calls the three Ts: tune in, talk more, and take turns. She notes:

> "Tune in" is sort of the most nuanced of the Ts. It's really seeing what your child's interested in, following your child's lead, using that child-directed speech, that sing-songy voice.

> "Talk more" is as it sounds—talking more, using rich vocabulary, narrating while you're changing your baby's diaper.

> And "take turns," which I think is the most powerful, is really viewing your child as a conversational partner. Even before they have a word or a babble, knowing that just by responding to any glances or gestures you're getting them ready to have a conversation and to do it from day one.

> And those three Ts are the foundation and the behavioral measuring stick that we should all use in interacting with our children.

Parents can and should extend learning at home by using these three Ts. Tuning in not only helps build vocabulary, it helps build your relationship with your child and, by example, teaches your child how to build relationships. Talking more provides the words your child needs to use to navigate the new and sometimes difficult emotions he or she experiences while learning and growing so rapidly. And taking turns shows your child that you want to continue the conversation and learn more, contributing to your child's sense of self-worth and value.

Chapter Sixteen

How Can I Help to Extend My Child's Learning in Later Schooling?

What we learn with pleasure, we never forget.
—Alfred Mercier

In *Visible Learners: Promoting Reggio-Inspired Approaches in All Schools*, the authors address the question of whether the overwhelming benefits of a Reggio-inspired, multifaceted, early learning environment can be obtained by children in elementary school, secondary school, and even graduate school. In particular, can the practice of making group learning visible through documentation be used effectively throughout a child's schooling? The answer is yes.

The best elementary and secondary school educators have developed strategies to create a powerful learning environment in which students construct their knowledge through meaningful relationships. For example:

- Teachers in a kindergarten classroom turned a conflict among children about the use of a scarce resource (a model yellow door) into an extended collaborative problem-solving project in which children were inspired to use negotiating, artistic, mathematical, scientific, engineering, and literacy skills to create and share more of the scarce resources.
- Kindergarten children engage in a lengthy, multifaceted project to study all aspects of the Boston Marathon, ultimately documenting their own learning through a video they created.
- A fourth-grade teacher develops an extended group learning experience about the physics of spinning materials that emerged "by accident" from the activities of children creating battling tops in their spare time.

- Seventh-grade English and science teachers collaborated to inspire a year-long cross-disciplinary inquiry into all of the dimensions and qualities of a nearby pond, leading to the development of writing, presenting, scientific reasoning, leadership, and citizenship skills.
- A high school AP English teacher encouraged students to understand multiple perspectives on the nature of human greatness revealed in literature by asking the students to document interviews with each other about that fundamental question.
- A high school math teacher encouraged students to work together outside the walls of the classroom on an extended project in which they designed, built, and presented a circus act, which demonstrated a complex quadratic equation involving gravity, velocity, and friction.
- Law school professors displayed the transformative power of true mathematics and literacy skills by bringing a basket of breadsticks to class and asking their students to develop an equitable method of sorting and dividing that scarce resource, and by bringing natural and repurposed materials and asking them to work together to design, construct, and advocate in favor of a model early-learning environment.

These are just a few examples of the shared projects created by educators who understand that true learning takes place when students are inspired to construct their knowledge in meaningful relationships with each other, teachers, and members of the surrounding community. They also demonstrate the power of documentation—of making the process and products of group learning visible through multiple forms of expression, including drawings, story acting, role-playing, puppetry, song, dance, clay, architecture, photos, and video. In an age in which accountability is demonstrated by standardized testing, documentation can provide to schools, families, and the community a true measure of student learning.

These particular examples of inspiring group learning and documentation at all education levels have one thing in common. Educators in these settings fully understand that learning is not the delivery of information from the teacher to students; rather, learning is a social process that results from relationships in and out of the classroom. Learning is not purely an objective intellectual exercise; rather, it is rooted in natural connections to people and materials including wonder, empathy, and joy. Learning is not the digestion and rote repeating of information; rather, learning is built upon the representation to others of evolving knowledge through multiple forms of expression; and learning is not passive; rather, learners take ownership in their own learning and believe in their own capacity to use their knowledge in the service of others.

In light of the value of extending these best practices beyond pre-K into the older years, families of pre-K children should work with educators at every level to support their use of these practices. One way to extend profound learning is for families to make the process and products of the child's early learning environment visible to educators in a school or educational institution. Educators in elementary school who observe the profound learning that takes place in a social constructivist early childhood education program will be inclined to engage in these best practices in their own classrooms.

Part III

How Do I Support All Our Children by Building Relationships with Other Families and the Community?

This final part provides to families, teachers, and administrators at all levels, as well as policymakers, methods of encouraging citizenship and building meaningful relationships throughout the community surrounding the school. It also demonstrates why each family benefits when all families have access to effective early childhood learning environments, and offers strategies for increasing that access for everyone.

Chapter Seventeen

How Can I Help My Child Develop as a Citizen, with the Power to Improve the World?

Those who are happiest are those who do the most for others.
—Booker T. Washington

A. CITIZENSHIP AND SERVICE PROJECTS

Early childhood education programs can incorporate community engagement and service learning into their educational experiences. In doing so, teachers develop each child's sense of identity, self-confidence, and relationship to his or her community and world. Providing such experiences empowers our youngest learners by giving them the opportunity to partner with their parents and other community members. It also enables them to develop their character as well as the competencies for citizenship in a democratic society.

Colonel Francis Wayland Parker was a bold educator who emphasized the importance of responsibility. Called "the father of progressive education" by John Dewey, Parker believed that educators should organize schools to meet the needs of society by engaging students along paths of inquiry generated in part by their own interests and curiosities. Accordingly, teachers can support the growth and development of the children in an early childhood education environment by making them aware of and responsive to the fundamental needs of society.

Teachers can thoughtfully incorporate various charitable acts into their curriculum. For example, early childhood programs can coordinate food, book, blanket, and toy drives. Children can show appreciation for senior citizens or veterans through activities such as performances at retirement communities or hospitals. Children can also initiate social endeavors such as fundraisers for organizations they are interested in supporting.

B. SCHOOL COLLABORATION

Early childhood education programs can inspire children to connect with their broader communities by engaging in interprogram collaborations. The shared activities between Winnetka Public School Nursery and Northwestern University Settlement House Head Start Preschool in the Chicago area are a model for this kind of cross-city collaboration. Although they are located in very different neighborhoods within the Chicagoland area, these schools designed a shared curriculum and connected their children through technology and periodic school visits. Working together with a shared studio art teacher (*atelierista*), children from both schools engaged in the same storytelling, sculpture, and drawing projects. They also worked together to develop documentation to make their shared learning visible to both communities. In so doing, the children and their families extended their perspectives well beyond their own neighborhoods, and grew to realize that they were contributing members and citizens of a wider community.

Schools can also work together in consortiums. A school consortium is an event typically offering several parent education events each year to address the most pressing social issues facing parents and their children. A school consortium's mission may be to promote integrity, responsibility, ethical behavior, and wellness in the school communities through ongoing collaboration and education. An example of a relevant topic featured at a school consortium would be how to raise thoughtful, self-reliant children.

By working together in consortiums, schools can also bring together children, parents, and educators from different areas to attend programs of common interest. A school consortium, for example, may pool resources to offer presentations to the wider community by thought leaders who address the most pressing social issues facing parents and their children. A wonderful example of such a consortium is the Family Action Network in the Chicago area, which connects parents, educators, and professionals through collaborative programming that educates, inspires, and positively impacts the broader community. The Family Action Network brings together people from all parts of Chicago, including parents from public, private, and parochial schools; educators and school administrators; and helping professionals. Through sponsorship and financial support from public school districts, private schools and organizations, area businesses, and faith communities, the Network is able to present renowned speakers free of charge on issues including education, parenting, and mental health. The Network not only serves the community, it also helps to build the community.

C. CONNECTING CHILDREN TO THE CITY THROUGH SHARED EXPLORATIONS

Some of the most effective early childhood education programs from throughout the world have collapsed the distinction between school and city by engaging both in shared explorations of a common question.

For example, in the early learning centers of Reggio Emilia, Italy, all members of the city are invited to investigate a single question for an entire year, or longer. One year's connective question, for example, might involve wheels, or bicycles, or chestnuts. Children in the early learning centers investigate the question along with adults in the city, and together they document their shared experience in investigating that particular topic.

That shared experience often results in new policy initiatives designed to solve problems encountered by all citizens of the city, from children to elders. The shared investigation of bicycles, for instance, led the children and the city to develop safer means of bicycle transportation. In addition, the city's walls, alleyways, and viaducts became filled with images and expressions of the shared exploration. Pictures of bicycles throughout the city serve as a constant reminder of the power of young children to effect lasting change.

Similarly, in the early childhood education programs provided for employees of Google, children work with adults in their surrounding community to pursue a common theme. One year, children at one of the early childhood sites became curious about why some kinds of leaves appear to have "lines" running up their spine. What emerged from their curiosity about those lines was an extended multigenerational communitywide exploration of the nature of lines in all of nature and human endeavor. Why do some leaves need lines of nourishment, and why do some human organizations need lines of authority? Citizens throughout that community documented their shared research into that common question.

Another such shared investigation pursued by Head Start programs in Chicago involved the nature of a "bridge." Children often encounter bridges large and small in their everyday lives. Many cities like Chicago rely on bridges to traverse waterways or railroad tracks. An early childhood program that inspires children to connect with community members around a shared investigation into various uses of bridges not only teaches children multiple learning strategies, it also makes their role as contributing citizens visible to the entire community.

Early learning connects children to their cities and gives them the power to engage their cities as fully respected citizens, capable of creating change. Mara Krechevsky, Ben Mardell, and Angela N. Romans suggest in their article, "Engaging City Hall: Children as Citizens," that current notions of advocacy in early childhood should be expanded to include this view—the view of children as citizens.

Early childhood advocates tackle very important issues, but often only from a needs-based perspective, where children are seen as passive and dependent on adults to ensure that these needs are met. Nurturing children's relationships with the community benefits both the children and the adults, who are encouraged to see the world in a new way. Krechevsky, Mardell, and Romans note that "when given the opportunity, children add a unique perspective about cultural, social, political, and moral questions to civic discourse."

As such: (1) the civic nature of schools should be highlighted; (2) there should be a focus on children's personalities and competencies rather than solely on their needs; (3) professional development should be provided for teachers around shared projects that promote higher-order thinking skills; and (4) children's learning should be documented to challenge assumptions about their capabilities.

D. OUTDOOR LEARNING

Among other things, being outside reduces anxiety, improves focus, and simply makes kids smarter.

In 2013, corporate director at a NASDAQ-traded firm and a former founder and CEO of Rubicon, Nilofer Merchant, created a stir when she noted that "sitting is the smoking of our generation." Months later, chairman emeritus of the Children & Nature Network and renowned author Richard Louv coined the term *nature-deficit disorder* to recognize the negative effects on children's well-being. He noted that, even in preschool, most children sit in the classroom for most of the day, and that in order to counteract the "business culture's bottom-line influence on education," it's important to provide for "far more activity, including unstructured play, to improve health, cognition and emotional well-being." Louv notes that "nature-based exercise appears to be especially effective. As a result, some pediatricians and mental health professionals are now prescribing 'green exercise' in parks and other natural settings."

Lawrence Rosen, MD, in his article "7 Science-Backed Reasons to Get Your Kids Outside," identified reasons why children should spend more time in nature. These include:

- It encourages exercise.
- It reduces anxiety: children in Maryland and Colorado who played in green schoolyards reported less stress than their peers.
- It improves focus: time spent outside leads to an attention boost.

- It makes kids smarter: children who are exposed to the outdoors more do better on cognitive tests.
- It builds a sense of community: children living in greener environments reported a stronger sense of "place."
- It helps develop connections with family: participating in camping experiences improves family relationships.
- It raises their interest in the environment: exposure to natural settings during childhood is associated with a greater interest in environmental stewardship.

Chapter Eighteen

What Is the Most Effective Way for Me to Make Sure That Other Children Have Access to Early Childhood Education?

I alone cannot change the world, but I can cast a stone across the waters to create many ripples.
—Mother Teresa

Chapter 18 respectfully suggests that each family should be engaged in efforts to increase access to effective early childhood education programs for their neighbors. Those efforts would help to bring true choice to all families in deciding how to provide early childhood education for their children, to achieve genuine coherence in learning approaches, and to foster and model meaningful relationships between families, schools, and communities.

A. WHY SHOULD I HELP INCREASE ACCESS FOR ALL CHILDREN?

Providing access to early childhood education programs would produce remarkable educational, social, and economic benefits for your children and for your neighbor's children. There is no doubt that the educational finance system in America creates wide disparities in the resources given to different districts and their children. On a federal level, there is not enough money to pay for indispensable programs such as special education services for children with disabilities. On a state and local level, the bulk of the money available to support education in America is derived from local property

155

taxes. School districts with high property wealth receive significantly more resources per child than districts with low property wealth.

As a result of this method of financing education, the median difference in per pupil expenditures between the wealthiest and poorest school districts in America is about $12,000 per child. Because neighborhoods are still generally segregated by race, and because most minority children reside in property-poor districts, the disparity in educational funding and in access to early childhood programs has an adverse impact on minority children.

And there is no doubt that money matters. Proponents of dismantling America's public education system sometimes argue that the public schools are a failure. The truth, however, is that many public schools are extremely successful by any measure. Students who attend public schools in property-rich districts and therefore receive sufficient resources not only outperform their charter and private school counterparts, they outperform children in comparable industrialized nations from throughout the world.

Many public schools in property-poor districts, on the other hand, simply do not receive sufficient funds to provide even a minimally adequate education for their students. The lack of resources in particular districts makes it extremely difficult for them to maintain healthy educational environments, to provide the instructional materials necessary to meet learning standards, to attract and retain qualified faculty and other educational professionals, and to sustain small classes, small schools, and tight teacher-student ratios. These are the most important ingredients of an effective education. Some public schools can afford them, but most schools cannot. Accordingly, the amount of resources allocated to educating each child in the early years is critical to that child's lifelong success and well-being.

Nonetheless, in an era of shrinking state and federal resources, efforts to increase the overall amount of public funds dedicated to education have not been widely successful. After all, why should the tax dollars taken from some families be shared with other families? In the absence of an overall increase in education funding, the process of removing inequities in education funding usually requires taking money from rich neighborhoods and sending it to poor neighborhoods. Even families that strongly believe in adequate education funding for all children may oppose measures that would reduce inequities by taking dollars from their own districts and sending them to different districts. Education funding is perceived to be a zero-sum game. If the pie is not increased, families in different districts are tempted to fight each other for their share.

An investment in early childhood education programs, however, would not be a zero-sum game. A substantial investment in effective early childhood education programs would actually increase educational revenue and reduce K–12 costs. It would increase the size of the pie for all families. In fact, the evidence is clear that every dollar invested in early childhood education programs would produce a return on that investment for the entire community of *at least* $7.

Wise families therefore recognize that the most cost-effective way to help their own children to grow up in a healthy, safe, and prosperous community is to support investments in early childhood education programs. All families have a shared interest in supporting such programs.

B. HOW DO I HELP? POLITICAL STRATEGIES TO INCREASE ACCESS

Increasing the availability of early childhood programs increases the choices available to all families with young children. There are national, state, local, and comprehensive political strategies for increasing access to early childhood education programs.

1. National Executive and Legislative Strategies

In the past decade, the president of the United States, officials in the U.S. Department of Education, and influential members of Congress have begun to recognize and advocate for access to effective pre-K programs for all children.

The federal government has made investments that work to expand access to early childhood programs, including developing partnerships with states to provide voluntary, full-day early childhood education programs for four-year-olds from low-income families.

In the Every Student Succeeds Act of 2015 (ESSA), Congress specifically authorizes the federal government to provide grant funds to the states that seek to enhance access to early childhood education programs for all children. The ESSA authorizes the federal government to reserve $250 million each year for Preschool Development Grants. Awarded through a competitive application process, states may use these funds to achieve four goals: improving early childhood education program coordination, easing the transition from preschool to kindergarten, improving parental choice, and sharing best practices among providers. Just like Head Start, the Preschool Development Grants will be administered primarily through the federal Department of Health and Human Services.

Any grants distributed through this process are awarded for one year and are renewable for up to three years. To compete for a grant, states must offer a mixed delivery system of early childhood education (i.e., a variety of options including Head Start, public school programs, and private childcare). States must also obtain at least 30 percent of the grant dollars from nonfederal sources. In addition to solidifying Preschool Development Grants, the

ESSA also mandates a review of all federal early childhood education programs.

Consistent with its K–12 provisions, ESSA prohibits the federal government from directly influencing state early childhood education standards. While ESSA preserves the federal role as a major funding source in early learning, it restricts its direct control to federally administered programs such as Head Start.

The ESSA, however, encourages innovation in, and growth of, early childhood education at programs at the state level. States have great freedom to spend their federal education dollars as they see fit under ESSA. In addition to participating in the Preschool Development Grant competition, states can choose to apply their general-purpose federal dollars to early childhood education; they do not need to restrict themselves to funding K–12 programs.

While federal funding remains intact, ESSA makes clear that expansion of access and improvement of quality in early childhood education will be driven primarily by the states. At the state level, wise and fiscally responsible policymakers will invest their scarce state resources in early childhood education programs because such an investment will yield the greatest return in the form of educational, social, and economic benefits and will actually generate additional revenue for the state.

Throughout the ESSA, Congress recognizes the consistently critical importance of early childhood education. But the federal law does not directly reserve any new funding for early learners. The $250 million that is set aside under ESSA amounts to only 0.35 percent of the $70.7 billion federal education budget.

To fully fund early childhood education programs for all four-year-olds, there would need to be an additional annual expense of $24 billion. Full funding of early childhood education programs for all three-year-olds would require an additional $28 billion, and thus full funding to provide outstanding early childhood education programs for all three- and four-year-olds would require a total additional annual expenditure of public funds of $52 billion.

Because these amounts are based on the assumption that all children would be enrolled in publicly funded programs and, in fact, many children would undoubtedly attend private pre-K programs, these estimates of the total additional funds needed to provide access to early childhood education programs for all three- and four-year-olds are significantly inflated. The actual expenditures would likely be less than these estimates.

Even these overestimated expenditures comprise only about eight percent of the total amount of the approximately $600 billion of public funds spent each year on the education of all elementary and secondary schoolchildren. The amount required to educate all three- and four-year-olds in America is far less than one percent of the entire federal budget.

2. State Strategies

The ESSA gives to the states the power and the incentives to increase access to early childhood programs. Mirroring the national focus on increasing access to early childhood education programs, many states have been considering creating and funding universal pre-K programs. States such as Oklahoma, Florida, New York, Indiana, and California have been particularly active in advocating universal pre-K programs for four-year-old children. Across the country, forty states offer a total of fifty-two state-funded pre-K programs, along with a program in the District of Columbia.

Oklahoma has become a model for statewide efforts to improve access to early childhood education. In 1998, Oklahoma became the second state to offer free, voluntary, early childhood education programs for the state's four-year-olds. As of 2012, the program is offered in 99 percent of the state's school districts. The program is funded through the state's school-funding formula, which is based on the age of the child and the length of the program day. In addition to public school settings, districts can also subcontract with other community programs, childcare centers, and Head Start settings, allowing districts to place public school teachers in those alternate settings. Students instructed in the alternate settings are still considered public school students. In 2011, Oklahoma again focused on pre-K education when its legislature passed a bill to require all students to be reading on grade level by the end of the third grade.

In a period of shrinking budgets and fiscal pressures, the states generally have reduced the funds allocated to early childhood education. They should be doing the opposite. As all of the economic evidence indicates, an investment in early childhood education programs saves costs, generates revenue, and yields robust returns. Such an investment is particularly necessary during periods of economic distress. States that wish to pursue prudent investments in early childhood education may take advantage of alternative funding strategies, including adding early childhood education programs to the state school-funding formula and creating Title I–supported early childhood education programs.

3. Local Strategies

New York City has developed and implemented a plan to offer pre-K to all four-year-olds by raising taxes for high-income residents. Pursuant to that plan, the city already has enrolled more than fifty thousand four-year-olds in early childhood education programs. Many of those children otherwise would not have had access to any prekindergarten education. Significantly, the city has determined that the most effective approach to early childhood education for all children requires training professional educators to use the social constructivist practices exemplified by the early learning centers of Reggio Emilia.

Similarly, in San Antonio, voters approved an eighth-of-a-cent sales tax increase to expand pre-K in 2012. This plan expands early childhood education programs to more than twenty-two thousand four-year-olds over the next eight years. In pushing for his plan, the mayor of San Antonio stressed the importance of a well-educated workforce for the future economic growth of the city, which helped to get the city's business community on board.

To win over taxpayers, city officials calculated the tax would cost the median household only $7.81 per year. The program garnered further political support by reserving 10 percent of the preschool slots for families who earn too much to qualify for free tuition. Finally, the program required the involvement of parents whose children attend the early childhood education programs to help counter critics who argued parents should be doing more.

4. Private Investments in Social Impact or Social Benefit Bonds

Another viable funding stream comes through that of private investments in social impact or social benefit bonds. Social impact or social benefit bonds are tools used to improve public services' outcomes, specifically those in disadvantaged populations, without burdening taxpayers. Social impact bonds, also known as "pay for success" programs, allow the government to pay for certain services, contingent on the success achieved by such services. Social impact bonds pay the public sector for their initial financing if the public sector reaches agreed-upon measurable outcomes.

In social impact bond agreements, the investor pays an external organization if the organization achieves specific agreed-upon measurable goals. If the organization reaches its goals, the government repays the organization's original investors. However, if the organization fails, the investors do not get repaid the government's funds, and the government is not responsible for any of the organization's debts.

In the fall of 2013, Utah received a social impact bond from Goldman Sachs and J. B. Pritzker to expand one of the state's early childhood education programs by 450 to 600 students, with the goal of reducing the need for costly special education services later in the students' academic careers. In this case, the investors will make money if the district meets its goals but will lose money if the district fails.

To identify students who are more likely to need special education services in the future, Utah's students are tested at the beginning of the program. Students will be tested again later, and for every student who scores at grade level, investors are paid back an amount equal to the avoided special education services cost. When the loan is completely paid, any additional money saved is split between the district and investors until students complete the sixth grade.

5. Developing Public-Private Partnerships to Expand Access to Early Childhood Education Programs

Another way to expand access to early childhood education programs is to develop public-private partnerships. From a legal standpoint, there is no question that a school district can lawfully allow a nondistrict provider of early childhood education programs to use its school facilities. A public school district may allow its property and facilities to be used or shared by nondistrict organizations. The district clearly has the power to partner with private and even religious providers of early childhood education.

From an economic standpoint, a school district's facilities typically are its most valuable resource. Where a district allows a private provider of pre-K education to use or share its facilities, it may receive a direct economic benefit by charging the provider for its use of those facilities.

Yet when a public school enables a private provider of early childhood education to use its facilities, it also reaps a more significant economic benefit. The children served by that private program will likely attend the district's schools when they reach kindergarten or first grade. By virtue of having a pre-K education, those children will not need as many district resources as they otherwise would have needed. The district's special education costs, health care costs, grade retention costs, and remediation costs will be substantially reduced.

From a political standpoint, the school district may want to present itself as an important part of the whole community. Consequently, the district may consider its physical assets to be those of the community at large. The district may even position its schools as the "hub of the community." Accordingly, another way in which a community can expand access to early childhood education programs—while reaping additional, communitywide benefits—is to create public-private partnerships.

6. The Comprehensive Strategy: Supporting Professional Educators

Families wishing to support the education of all of their children might want to consider a comprehensive approach. They can do this by supporting a culture in which teachers are valued and held accountable through a range of authentic assessment tools, including documentation.

Finland provides a particularly compelling model for communities seeking to expand access to early childhood educational opportunities. In *Finnish Lessons: What Can the World Learn from Educational Change in Finland?* (2011), Pasi Sahlberg describes how Finland transformed its educational system into a paragon of excellence and equity—during a period of tremendous economic distress.

As a result of its national reform initiatives, Finland is one of the world's leaders in the academic performance of its secondary school students. Finnish schools seem to serve all students well, regardless of background, status, or ability. Experts recognize that the strength of Finland's school system is its equitably distributed high level of student learning. According to virtually every international indicator of educational quality, Finland now "has one of the most educated citizenries in the world, provides educational opportunities in an egalitarian manner, and makes efficient use of resources."

In particular, data and surveys from the Organization for Economic Cooperation and Development (OECD), Trends in International Mathematics and Sciences Study (TMSS), and the International Programme for Student Assessment (PISA) show that Finnish students excel in educational performance over all assessed domains, including math, literacy, and science. In the Global Index of Cognitive Skills and Educational Attainment, which compares performance on international education tests, literacy, and graduation rates for students from forty industrialized countries, Finland ranks at or near the top and well ahead of the United States.

Moreover, Finland has accomplished this remarkable level of student learning in an extremely cost-efficient manner. Although virtually all of Finland's expenditures for education derive from public funds, its total educational expenditures are only 5.6 percent of its gross domestic product. That percentage is less than the average spent by the other highest-performing countries, and substantially less than America's rate of 7.6 percent of gross domestic product. Significantly, the cumulative cost of educating a student from ages six to fifteen in Finland is approximately 60 percent of the cost of educating such a student in the United States.

What are the particular educational reforms that have led to Finland's remarkable success? Educators from all over the world have studied the Finnish experience and have settled on five critical ingredients:

1. Equal educational opportunities are available for all, including early childhood education resources.
2. Teaching is a revered and highly valued profession to which the best and brightest students aspire.
3. Parents, students, and political figures trust teachers and school administrators, and give them professional freedom to develop and adjust their skills to meet student needs.
4. The political forces surrounding education maintain a stable vision of education as a public service, and defer to the professional judgments of educators to implement that vision.

5. The nation has not fallen prey to the fallacious educational "account-ability" movement rooted in externally imposed, high-stakes standard-ized tests.

Among these characteristics, the most important factor is that of the daily hard work of excellent teachers. The development of an excellent and equita-ble national system of early childhood education starts with improving teach-er education. The Finnish experience "shows that it is more important to ensure that teachers' work in schools is based on professional dignity and social respect . . . Teachers' work should strike a balance between classroom teaching and collaboration with other professionals in school."

As Sahlberg and virtually all serious education experts throughout the world who have studied Finland have concluded, "All of the factors that are behind the Finnish success seem to be the opposite of what is taking place in the United States." Finland has rejected the American strategies of test-based accountability, standardization, privatization, charter schools, school clos-ings, and belittling teachers and their unions. Instead of pursuing these poli-cies, Finland has achieved its remarkable educational improvement by in-vesting public funds wisely in a system that trains and trusts its professional educators to teach all of its children to develop habits of mind vital to their future.

Reliance on Finland as a guide to educational reform in the United States has been criticized on the grounds that Finland is a relatively small country with a homogeneous population. Yet the reforms that have driven Finland's success have been employed with similar results throughout the world. In *The Learning Curve*, the Economist Intelligence Unit analyzed data from over forty countries to determine the strength of correlation between educa-tion reforms and nationwide student outcomes.

Data reveal lessons for early education policymakers in the United States. Five strategies are indispensable to effective early childhood education pro-grams: (1) a long-term investment and a sustained systemwide approach; (2) support for the value of education for all children within the surrounding culture; (3) collaboration with—not control by—parents and caregivers; (4) instructional practices and goals designed to teach children skills and habits of mind they will need for the future, not the past; and (5) a systemic com-mitment to respecting and valuing early childhood educators as profession-als.

In particular, the report found: "There is no substitute for good teach-ers. . . . Successful school systems have a number of things in common: they find culturally effective ways to attract the best people to the profession; they provide relevant, ongoing training; they give teachers a status similar to that of other respected professions; and the system sets clear goals and expecta-tions but also lets teachers get on with meeting these." The remarkably diverse group of countries that have achieved educational excellence all share Finland's commitment to valuing teachers as professionals and to granting them the autonomy to collaborate with their colleagues in educating their students according to their professional judgment.

By pursuing this comprehensive strategy—or any combination of effective strategies to expand access to pre-K programs—families would help to produce substantial educational, social, and economic benefits for all children, regardless of their race, ethnicity, or socioeconomic status. The investment of resources in early childhood education for each child would provide remarkable lifelong benefits for all of our children.

Conclusion

And thus they tell the child / that the hundred is not there. / The child says: /
No way. The hundred is there.
—Loris Malaguzzi

Through the pages of this book, we have had the honor and privilege of accompanying you as you make an incredibly important decision: Which early childhood education program is best for your family?

We realize that this decision is an incredibly personal one, which requires a delicate balance of many factors. And we trust that each family will weigh these factors in a way that works best for them.

As you weigh those factors, however, we hope that you will be guided and supported by the research, experiences, and best practices this Companion offers. Apart from the many practical concerns such as convenience and cost, we hope that you will search for and partner with an early childhood program that:

- Takes a social constructivist approach to early childhood education in which respected and valued teachers, themselves lifelong learners, guide children in their play and encourage them to build their own knowledge by constructing meaningful relationships.
- Does not make misguided claims about making children "kindergarten ready" by inappropriately preparing them to perform traditional academic skills that are measured on standardized tests.
- Follows positive approaches to discipline based upon the model of restorative justice.
- Provides special education and related services to children with special needs and fully includes those children in the learning environment.

- Appreciates and supports the home languages spoken by children and embraces those languages together with English in the learning environment.
- Includes and celebrates as a tremendous strength children from diverse racial, ethnic, and economic backgrounds.
- Makes your child's learning visible through documentation.
- Appreciates your child's family as an essential partner in the learning process.
- Inspires your entire family to connect the learning that takes place in the early childhood education program with the well-being of the community.
- Recognizes that there's no learning without joy.

Enrolling in a program with these attributes might not be easy. Many such programs exist, and they are likely to be convenient and affordable. But parents might be tempted to discard the benefits of these kinds of programs in favor of programs that try to sell the kind of short-term benefits that can be measured in a test score.

As your Companion, we urge you to avoid that temptation. The early years last forever. Parenting is not a quick-fix, short-term relationship. Rather, with the support of this book, we trust that families will choose an early childhood education program that leads to lifelong learning, professional success, and well-being. Such a program is one in which you and your child become partners in a diverse learning community guided by highly respected teachers who inspire children to construct their own knowledge by building meaningful and sustainable relationships with adults, peers, and the community.

Appendix

Early Childhood Education Program Rubric

Table 18.1.

Factor	Sch. #1	Sch. #2	Sch. #3	Sch. #4	Sch. #5
Social Constructivist Approach?					
Cost: Affordable?					
Image of Child: Caring, Capable?					
Goal: Learning Community?					
Teachers: Highly Qualified and Valued?					
Role of Family: Partners?					
Diversity: Celebrated?					
Learning: Made Visible?					
Education Purpose: Collaborative, Innovators?					
Discipline: Restorative?					
Special Needs: Inclusive?					
Different Learning: Respected?					
Social and Emotional Growth: Valued?					
Interactions: Connected to Children?					
Schedule of Days/Hours: Meets Our Needs?					
Location: Convenient and Connected?					
Environment: Itself Is a Teacher?					
Warmth: Obvious and Abundant?					

LEGEND

S—Strength
W—Weakness
N—Neither a strength nor a weakness
Sch. = School

References

Chapter 1

Aud, Susan, Sidney Wilkinson-Flicker, Paul Kristapovich, Amy Rathbun, Xiaolei Wang, and Barnett, W. S. "Effectiveness of Early Educational Intervention." *Science* 333 (2011): 975–78.

Behrman, J. R., Y. Cheng, and P. E. Todd. "Evaluating Preschool Programs When Length of Exposure to the Program Varies: A Nonparametric Approach." *Review of Economics and Statistics* 86(1) (2004): 108–32.

Berlinski, S., S. Galiani, and P. Gertler. "The Effect of Pre-Primary Education on Primary School Performance." *Journal of Public Economics* 93 (2009): 219–34.

Berlinski, S., S. Galiani, and M. Manacorda. "Giving Children a Better Start: Preschool Attendance and School-Age Profiles." *Journal of Public Economics* 92 (2008): 1416–40.

Camilli, G., Sadako Vargas, Sharon Ryan, and W. Steven Barnett. "Meta-Analysis of the Effects of Early Education Interventions on Cognitive and Social Development." *Teachers College Record* 112(3) (2010): 579–620.

Committee for Economic Development. "Early Education—Preschool for All: Investing in a Productive and Just Society." 2002.

Diamond, A. and K. Lee. "Interventions Shown to Aid Executive Function Development in Children 4 to 12 Years Old." *Science* 333 (2011): 959–64.

Gorkey, Kevin. "Early Childhood Education: A Meta-Analytic Affirmation of the Short- and Long-Term Benefits of Educational Opportunity." *School Psychology Quarterly* 16(1) (2001): 9–30.

Haynes, T. and M. Mogstad. "No Child Left Behind: Subsidized Child Care and Children's Long-Run Outcomes." *American Economic Journal: Economic Policy* 3(2) (2011): 97–129.

Heckman, James J. "Schools, Skills, and Synapses." *Economic Inquiry* 46 (2008).

Schweinhart, Lawrence J., Jeanne Montie, Zongping Xiang, W. Steven Barnett, Clive R. Belfield, and Milagros Nores. *The High/Scope Perry Preschool Study through Age 40*. Ypsilanti: HighScope Press, 2005.

Schweinhart, Lawrence J. and David P. Weikart. "The HighScope Model of Early Childhood Education." In *Approaches to Early Childhood Education*, eds. Jaipaul L. Roopnarine and James E. Johnson. Boston: Pearson, 2013.

Zhang, Jijun. *The Condition of Education 2013*. Washington, DC: U.S. Department of Education, 2013.

Chapter 2

Barnett, W. Steven, Megan E. Carolan, Jen Fitzgerald, and James H. Squires. *The State of Preschool 2013: State Preschool Yearbook*. New Brunswick, NJ: National Institute for Early Education Research, 2013.

Barth, Patte. "Invest in Pre-K: Win Valuable Prizes." Presentation at Loyola University Chicago School of Law Early Childhood Education Symposium, Chicago, Illinois, March 15, 2013. Accessed January 4, 2016. http://www.luc.edu/law/centers/childlaw/institutes/child_education/symposium.html.

45 C.F.R. Section 1304.21 (2007).

Hager, Maureen. "Implementing the Vision: Strategies for Creating Lawful, High-Quality, and Cost-Effective Early Childhood Collaborations." Presentation at Loyola University Chicago School of Law Early Childhood Education Symposium, Chicago, Illinois, March 15, 2013. Accessed January 4, 2016. http://www.luc.edu/law/centers/childlaw/institutes/child_education/symposium.html.

Head Start, An Office of the Administration for Children and Families Early Childhood Learning & Knowledge Center (ECLKC). "Head Start Program Facts, Fiscal Year 2012." Accessed January 4, 2016. http://eclkc.ohs.acf.hhs.gov/hslc/mr/factsheets/docs/hs-program-fact-sheet-2012.pdf.

Individuals with Disabilities Act 2004, Part B, §619.

Mead, Sarah. "Why Are These Kids so Short? An Introduction to Early Childhood Education." Presentation at Loyola University Chicago School of Law Early Childhood Education Symposium, Chicago, Illinois, March 15, 2013. Accessed January 4, 2016. http://www.luc.edu/law/centers/childlaw/institutes/child_education/symposium.html.

Powell, Douglas R. "The Head Start Program." In *Approaches to Early Childhood Education*, eds. Jaipaul L. Roopnarine and James E. Johnson. Boston: Pearson, 2013.

U.S. Department of Education, National Center for Education Statistics, Digest of Education Statistics. "Table 202.10: Enrollment of 3-, 4-, and 5-year old Children in Primary Programs, by Level of Program, Control of Program, and Attendance Status: Selected Years, 1965 through 2012." Washington, DC: U.S. Department of Education, 2013. Accessed January 4, 2016. http://nces.ed.gov/programs/digest/d13/tables/dt13_202.10.asp.

U.S. Department of Health & Human Services, Office of the Assistant Secretary for Planning and Evaluation. "2013 Poverty Guidelines." Accessed January 4, 2016. https://aspe.hhs.gov/2013-poverty-guidelines -guidelines.

Chapter 3

Berk, L. E., T. D. Mann, and A. T. Ogan. "Make-Believe Play: Wellspring for Development of Self-Regulation." In *Play = Learning: How Play Motivates and Enhances Cognitive and Social-Emotional Growth*, eds. Dorothy G. Singer, Roberta Michnick Golinkoff, and Kathryn A. Hirsh-Pasek. New York: Oxford University Press, 2006.

Bodrova, Elena and Leong, Deborah J. "Tools of the Mind: The Vygotskian Approach." In *Approaches to Early Childhood Education*, eds. Jaipaul L. Roopnarine and James E. Johnson. Boston: Pearson, 2013.

Chertoff, Emily. "Reggio Emilia: From Postwar Italy to NYC's Toniest Preschools." *The Atlantic*, January 17, 2013.

Davilla, Donna E. and Susan M. Koenig. "Bringing the Reggio Concept to American Educators." *Art Education* 51(18) (1998): 19.

Filippini, T. "Introduction to the Reggio Approach." Paper presented at the annual conference of the National Association for the Education of Young Children, Washington DC, November 1990.

Forman, G. and B. Fyfe. "Negotiated Learning Through Design, Documentation and Discourse." In *The Hundred Languages of Children: The Reggio Emilia Approach—Advanced Reflections*, eds. Carolyn Edwards, Lella Gandini, and George Forman. Greenwich, CT: Ablex, 1998.

Gandini, Lella. "History, Ideas, and Basic Principles: An Interview with Loris Malaguzzi." In *The Hundred Languages of Children*, eds. Carolyn Edwards, Lella Gandini, and George Forman. Santa Barbara: Praeger, 2012.

Gandini, Lella and J. Goldhaber. "Two Reflections about Documentation," in *Bambini: The Italian Approach to Infant/Toddler Care*, eds. Lella Gandini and Carolyn Edwards. New York: Teachers College Press, 2001.

Gandini, Lella, Lynn Hill, Louise Cadwell, and Charles Schwall. *In the Spirit of the Studio: Learning from the Atelier of Reggio Emilia*. New York: Teachers College Press, 2005.

Grabell, Matthew. "Should More American Preschools Take a Lesson from Google? An Analysis of Reggio Emilia Preschools and Their Impact on a Child's Life." *Loyola University Chicago Journal of Early Education Law and Policy* (2012).

Hertzog, Nancy B. "Reflections and Impressions from Reggio Emilia: 'It's Not about Art!'" *Early Childhood Research & Practice* 3(1) (2001).

Hewett, Valarie Mercilliott. "Examining the Reggio Emilia Approach to Early Childhood Education." *Early Childhood Education Journal* 29(95) (2001): 96–97.

Hinckle, Pia. "The Best Schools in the World." *Newsweek*, December 2, 1991.

Karpov, Yuriy V. *The Neo-Vygotsky Approach to Child Development*. Boston: Cambridge University Press, 2005.

Kozulin, Alex. *Vygotsky's Psychology: A Biography of Ideas*. Boston: Cambridge University Press, 1990.

Linn, Margaret Inman. "An American Educator Reflects on the Meaning of the Reggio Experience." *Phi Delta Kappan* 83(332) (2001): 333–34.

Malaguzzi, Loris. "No Way. The Hundred Is There." In *The Hundred Languages of Children*, eds. Carolyn Edwards, Lella Gandini, and George Forman, translated by Lella Gandini. Santa Barbara: Praeger, 2012.

New, Rebecca S. "Theory and Praxis in Reggio Emilia: They Know What They Are Doing, and Why." In *The Hundred Languages of Children: The Reggio Emilia Approach—Advanced Reflections*, eds. Carolyn Edwards, Lella Gandini, and George Forman. Greenwich, CT: Ablex, 1998.

New, Rebecca S. "Culture, Child Development and Developmentally Appropriate Practices. Teachers As Collaborative Researchers," in *Diversity and Developmentally Appropriate Practices: Challenges for Early Childhood Education*, eds. B. Mallory and Rebecca S. New. New York: Teachers College Press, 1994.

New, Rebecca S. "Reggio Emilia as Cultural Activity Theory in Practice." *Theory into Practice* 46(1) (2007): 5, 6.

New, Rebecca S. and Rebecca Kantor. "Reggio Emilia in the 21st Century: Enduring Commitments Amid New Challenges." In *Approaches to Early Childhood Education*, eds. Jaipaul L. Roopnarine and James E. Johnson. New York: Pearson, 2013.

Rinaldi, Carlina. "The Emergent Curriculum and Social Constructivism." In *The Hundred Languages of Children: The Reggio Emilia Approach to Early Childhood Education*, eds. Carolyn Edwards, Lella Gandini, and George Forman. Norwood, NJ: Ablex, 1993.

Rinaldi, Carlina. *In Dialogue with Reggio Emilia: Listening, Researching, and Learning* (Contesting Early Childhood Series). New York: Routledge, 2006.

Rinaldi, Carlina. "Projected Curriculum Constructed through Documentation—*Progettazione*: An Interview with Lella Gandini," in *The Hundred Languages of Children: The Reggio Emilia Approach—Advanced Reflections*, eds. Carolyn Edwards, Lella Gandini, and George Forman. Greenwich, CT: Ablex, 1998.

Rinaldi, Carlina. "The Teacher as Researcher." *Innovations in Early Education: The International Reggio Exchange* 10(2) (2003): 1–4.

Roopnarine, Jaipaul L. and James E. Johnson, eds. *Approaches to Early Childhood Education*. Boston: Pearson, 2013.

Scheinfield, Daniel R., Karen M. Haigh, and Sandra J. P. Scheinfeld. *We Are All Explorers, Learning and Teaching with Reggio Principles in Urban Settings*. New York: Teachers College Press, 2008.

Soncini, Ivana. "The Inclusive Community." In *The Hundred Languages of Children: The Reggio Emilia Experience in Transformation*, eds. Carolyn Edwards, Lella Gandini, and George Forman. Santa Barbara: Praeger, 2012.

Topal, C. and L. Gandini. *Beautiful Stuff!: Learning with Found Materials*. St. Paul, MN: Redleaf Press, 1999.

Torrence, Martha and John Chattin-McNichols. "Montessori Education Today." In *Approaches to Early Childhood Education* , eds. Roopnarine and Johnson, 359, citing Maria Montessori, *The Absorbent Mind*. New York: Dell, 1967a, originally published 1949.

Wexler, Alice. "A Theory for Living: Walking with Reggio Emilia." *Art Education* 57(13) (2004): 13–16.

Wood, D., J. S. Bruner, and G. Ross. "The Role of Tutoring in Problem Solving." *Journal of Child Psychology and Psychiatry* 17(2) (1976).

Chapter 4

Almon, Joan. *Adventure: The Value of Risk in Children's Play*. Annapolis: Alliance for Childhood, 2013.

Barnett, W. S. "Effectiveness of Early Educational Intervention." *Science* 333 (2011): 975–78.

Barnett, W. S., Kwanghee Jung, Donald J. Yarosz, Jessica Thomas, Amy Hornbeck, Robert Stechuk, Susan Burns, and George Mason University. "Educational Effects of the Tools of the Mind Curriculum: A Randomized Trial." *Early Childhood Research Quarterly* 23 (2008): 299–313.

Barnett, W. S. and L. N. Masse. "Early Childhood Program Design and Economic Returns: Comparative Benefit-Cost Analysis of the Abecedarian Program and Its Policy Complications." *Economics of Education Review* 26 (2007): 113–25.

Barresi, John and Chris Moore. "The Neuroscience of Social Understanding." In *The Shared Mind: Perspectives on Intersubjectivity*, eds. Jordan Zlatev et al. Amsterdam: John Benjamins Publishing Company, 2008.

Behrman, J. R., Y. Cheng, and P. E. Todd. "Evaluating Preschool Programs When Length of Exposure to the Program Varies: A Nonparametric Approach." *Review of Economics and Statistics* 86(1) (2004): 108–32.

Belfield, C., M. Nores, W. S. Barnett, and L. J. Schweinhart. "The High/Scope Perry Preschool Program." *Journal of Human Resources* 41(1) (2006): 162–90.

Berk, Laura E. and Adam Winsler. *Scaffolding Children's Learning: Vygotsky and Early Childhood Education*. National Association for the Education of Young Children, 1995.

Berlinski, S., S. Galiani, and P. Gertler. "The Effect of Pre-Primary Education on Primary School Performance." *Journal of Public Economics* 93 (2009): 219–34.

Berlinski, S., S. Galiani, and M. Manacorda. "Giving Children a Better Start: Preschool Attendance and School-Age Profiles." *Journal of Public Economics* 92 (2008): 1416–40.

Bonawitz, Elizabeth, Patrick Shafto, Hyowon Gweon, Noah D. Goodman, Elizabeth Spelke, and Laura Shulz. "The Double-Edged Sword of Pedagogy: Instruction Limits Spontaneous Exploration and Discovery." *Cognition* 120(3) (2011): 322–30.

Borghans, Lex, Bart H. H. Golsteyn, James Heckman, and John Eric Humphries. "Identification Problems in Personality Psychology." *Personality and Individual Differences*, 51(3) (2011): 315–20.

Borghans, Lex, Angela Lee Duckworth, James J. Heckman, and Bas ter Weel. "The Economics and Psychology of Personality Traits." *The Journal of Human Resources* 43 (2000): 972–1050.

Borghans, Les, Bas ter Weel, and Bruce A. Weinberg. "Interpersonal Styles and Labor Market Outcomes." Working Paper, National Bureau of Economic Research, January 2007. Accessed January 5, 2016. http://www.nber.org/papers/w12846.pdf.

Brooks-Gunn, Jeanne Kathryn Duckworth, and Crista Japel. "School Readiness and Later Achievement." *Developmental Psychology* 43(6) (2007): 1428–46.

Camilli, G., Sadako Vargas, Sharon Ryan, and W. Steven Barnett. "Meta-Analysis of the Effects of Early Education Interventions on Cognitive and Social Development." *Teachers College Record* 112(3) (2010): 579–620.

Committee on Integrating the Science of Early Childhood Development. *From Neurons to Neighborhoods: The Science of Early Childhood Development*, eds. Jack P. Shonkoff and Deborah A. Phillips. Washington, DC: National Academy Press, 2000.

Diamond, Adele, W. Steven Barnett, Jessica Thomas, and Sarah Munro. "Preschool Program Improves Cognitive Control." *Science* 318(5855) (November 2007): 1387–88.

Diamond, Adele and K. Lee. "Interventions Shown to Aid Executive Function Development in Children 4 to 12 Years Old." *Science* 333 (2011): 959–64.

Dickerson, Sally S. and Peggy M. Zoccola. "Towards a Biology of Social Support." In *The Oxford Handbook of Positive Psychology*, eds. Shane J. Lopez and C. R. Snyder. New York: Oxford University Press, 2009.

Diener, Ed and Robert Biswas-Diener. *Happiness: Unlocking the Mysteries of Psychological Wealth*. Malden, MA: Wiley-Blackwell, 2008.

Diener, Ed and Martin E. P. Seligman. "Very Happy People." *Psychological Science* 13(1) (January 2002).

Duncan, Greg J., Amy Claessens, Aletha C. Huston, Linda S. Pagani, Mimi Engel, Holly Sexton, Chantelle J. Dowsett, Katherine Magnuson, Pamela Klebanov, Leon Feinstein, Jeanne Durlak, et al. "The Impact of Student's Social and Emotional Learning: A Meta-Analysis of School-Based Universal Interventions." *Child Development* 82(1) (2011): 405–32.

Gardner, Howard. *Five Minds for the Future*. Boston: Harvard Business Review Press, 2008.

Gorkey, Kevin. "Early Childhood Education: A Meta-Analytic Affirmation of the Short- and Long-Term Benefits of Educational Opportunity." *School Psychology Quarterly* 16(1) (2001): 9–30.

Guttmann-Steinmetz, S. and J. A. Cromwell. "Attachment and Externalizing Disorders: A Developmental Psychopathology Perspective." *Journal of the American Academy of Child & Adolescent Psychiatry* 45(4) (2006).

Havnes, T. and M. Mogstad. "No Child Left Behind: Subsidized Child Care and Children's Long-Run Outcomes." *American Economic Journal: Economic Policy* 3(2) (2011): 97–129.

Hawkins, David. "I, Thou and It." In *The Informed Vision: Essays on Learning and Human Nature*. New York: Agathon Press, 2002.

Heckman, James J. *Giving Kids a Fair Chance (A Strategy That Works)*. Cambridge, MA: The MIT Press/Boston Review Books, 2014.

Heckman, James J. "School, Skills and Synapses." Working Paper, National Bureau of Economic Research, June 2008, 21. Accessed January 5, 2016. http://www.nber.org/papers/w14064.pdf.

Heckman, James J. "Schools, Skills, and Synapses." *Economic Inquiry* 46 (2008).

Heckman, James J. and Tim Kautz. "Fostering and Measuring Skills: Interventions That Improve Character and Cognition." Working Paper, National Bureau of Economic Research, 2013. Accessed January 5, 2016. http://www.nber.org/papers/w19656.pdf.

Heckman, James J. and Tim Kautz. "Hard Evidence on Soft Skills." National Bureau of Edonomic Research Working Paper Series (2012), 3.

Heckman, James J., Rodrigo Pinto, and Peter Savelyev. "Understanding the Mechanisms through Which an Influential Early Childhood Program Boosted Adult Outcomes." *The American Economic Review* 103(6) (2013): 2052–86.

Heckman, James and Lakshmi Raut. "Long-Term Effects of Preschool-Structural Estimates from a Discrete Programming Model." Working Paper, National Bureau of Economic Research, 2013. Accessed January 5, 2016. http://www.nber.org/papers/w19077.pdf.

Heckman, James J. and Yona Rubinstein. "The Importance of Noncognitive Skills: Lessons from the G.E.D. Testing Program." *American Economics Review* 91(2) (2001): 145–49.

Heckman, James J., Jora Stixrud, and Sergio Urzua. "The Effects of Cognitive and Noncognitive Abilities on Labor Market Outcomes and Social Behavior." Working Paper, National Bureau of Economic Research, 2006. Accessed January 5, 2016. http://www.nber.org/papers/w12006.pdf.

Holder, Mark D. and Ben Coleman. "The Contribution of Social Relationships to Children's Happiness." *Journal of Happiness Studies* 10 (2007): 329–49.

Kahneman, Daniel. *Thinking, Fast and Slow*. New York: Farrar, Straus and Giroux, 2011.

Kahneman, Daniel, Alan B. Kruger, David A. Schkade, Norbert Schwarz, and Arthur A. Stone. "A Survey Method for Characterizing Daily Life Experience: The Day Reconstruction Method." *Science* 306(5702) (2004): 1776–80.

Kaye, Kenneth. *The Mental and Social Life of Babies*. Chicago: University of Chicago Press, 1992.

Kohn, Alfie. "Appendix A, The Hard Evidence: Early Childhood Education: The Case Against Direct Instruction of Academic Skills." In *The Schools Our Children Deserve*. Boston: Houghton Mifflin, 2009.

Lewin-Benham, Ann. *Twelve Best Practices for Early Childhood Education: Integrating Reggio and Other Inspired Approaches*. New York: Teachers College Press, 2011.

Mardell, Ben and Rachel Carbonara. "A Research Project on the Reggio Emilia Approach and Children's Learning Outcomes." *Innovations in Education* (Summer 2013): 6.

Montie, Jeanne E., Zongping Xiang, and Lawrence Schweinhart. "Preschool Experience in 10 Countries: Cognitive and Language Performance at Age 7." *Early Childhood Research Quarterly* 21 (2005): 313–31.

National Scientific Council on the Developing Child and National Forum on Early Childhood Policy and Programs. "Building the Brain's 'Air Traffic Control' System: How Early Experiences Shape the Development of Executive Function." Working Paper no. 11, Harvard University Center on the Developing Child, 2011.

Papousek, H. and M. Papousek "Intuitive Parenting: A Dialectic Counterpart to the Infant's Integrative Compliance." In *Handbook of Infant Development*, ed. J. D. Osofsky. New York: Wiley, 1987.

Pardo, Laura. "What Every Teacher Needs to Know About Comprehension." *International Reading Association* 58 (2004): 276.

Perry, Bruce and Annette Jackson. "The Long and Winding Road: From Neuroscience to Policy, Program, Practice." *Victorian Council of Social Services Journal* 9 (2014): 4–8.

Pink, Daniel. *A Whole New Mind: Why Right-Brainers Will Rule the Future*. New York: Riverhead Books, 2006.

Ramachandram, Vilayanur S. *The Tell-Tale Brain: A Neuroscientist's Quest for What Makes Us Human*. New York: W. W. Norton & Company, 2010.

Roberts, Brent W., Nathan R. Kuncel, Rebecca Shiner, Avshalom Caspi, and Lewis R. Goldberg. "The Power of Personality: The Comparative Validity of Personality Traits, Socioeconomic Status, and Cognitive Ability for Predicting Important Life Outcomes." *Perspectives in Psychological Sciences* 2(4) (2007): 313–45.

Robinson, Maria. *From Birth to One: The Year of Opportunity*. Buckingham: Open University Press, 2003.

Schweinhart, Lawrence J., Jeanne Montie, Zongping Xiang, W. Steven Barnett, Clive R. Belfield, and Milagros Nores. *Lifetime Effects: The HighScope Perry Preschool Study through Age 40*. Ypsilanti: HighScope Press, 2005.

Schweinhart, Lawrence J. and David P. Weikart. "The HighScope Model of Early Childhood Education." In *Approaches to Early Childhood Education*, eds. Jaipaul L. Roopnarine and James E. Johnson. Boston: Pearson, 2013.

Schweinhart, Lawrence J. and David P. Weikart. *Lasting Differences: The HighScope Preschool Model Comparison Study through Age 23*. Ypsilanti, MI: HighScope Press, 1997.

Seligman, Martin E. P. *Flourish: A Visionary New Understanding of Happiness and Well-Being*. New York: Free Press, 2011.

Siegel, Daniel. *The Developing Mind: Towards a Neurobiology of Interpersonal Experience*. New York: Guilford Press, 1999.

Siegel, Daniel J. *Mindsight: The New Science of Personal Transformation*. New York: Bantam Books, 2011, 40.

Szalavitz, Maia and Bruce D. Perry, *Born of Love: Why Empathy Is Essential—and Endangered*. New York: HarperCollins, 2010.

Temple, J. A. and A. J. Reynolds. "Benefits and Costs of Investments in Preschool Education: Evidence from the Child-Parent Centers and Related Programs." *Economics of Education Review* 26(1) (2007): 126–44.

Tomer, John F. "Adverse Childhood Experiences, Poverty, and Inequality: Toward an Understanding of the Connections and the Cures." *World Economic Review* 3(20) (2014): 20–36.

Tough, Paul. *How Children Succeed: Grit, Curiosity, and the Hidden Power of Character.* London: Random House, 2013.

Vygotsky, Lev. *Mind in Society: The Development of Psychological Processes.* Boston: Harvard University Press, 1978.

Vygotsky, Lev. "Play and Its Role in the Mental Development of the Child." *Soviet Psychology* 5 (1933).

Welsh, Janet A., Robert L. Nix, Clancy Blair, Karen L. Bierman, and Keith E. Nelson. "The Development of Cognitive Skills and Gains in Academic School Readiness for Children from Low-Income Families." *Journal of Educational Psychology* 102(1) (2010): 43–53.

Yoshikawa, Hirokazu, Christina Weiland, Jeanne Brooks-Gunn, Margaret R. Burchinal, Linda M. Espinosa, William T. Gormley, Jens Ludwig, Katherine A. Magnuson, Deborah Phillips, and Martha J. Zaslow. *Investing in Our Future: The Evidence Base on Preschool Education.* The Society for Research in Child Development, Foundation for Child Development, October 2013.

Chapter 5

American Academy of Pediatrics. "Corporal Punishment in Schools." *Pediatrics* 106(343) (August 2000).

Anderson, Melinda D. "Why Are So Many Preschoolers Getting Suspended?" *The Atlantic,* December 7, 2015.

Burwell, Sylvia M. and Arne Duncan. "United States Department of Health and Human Services and United States Department of Education Joint Letter." December 10, 2014. https://www.acf.hhs.gov/sites/default/files/ecd/hhs_and_ed_joint_letter.pdf.

Guthrow, J. "Correlation Between High Rates of Corporal Punishment in Public Schools and Social Pathologies." *Parents and Teachers Against Violence in Education*, 2002. Accessed January 5, 2016. http://www.nospank.net/correlationstudy.htm.

Holland, Jesse J. and Kimberly Hefling. "Thousands of Preschool Kids Face Suspension." *Associated Press: Big Story*, March 21, 2014.

Illinois Transforming School Discipline Collaborative. "Draft Model Code of Conduct for Review and Feedback."

National Association of School Psychologists. "NASP Position Statement: Corporal Punishment." NASP: Bethesda, MD, 2011. 105 ILCS 5/27 23.7(b)(12).

Chapter 6

Epstein, Ann S. "Using Technology Appropriately in the Preschool Classroom." *HighScope Extensions* (28). Accessed January 5, 2016. http://www.highscope.org/file/NewsandInformation/Extensions/ExtVol28No1_highres.pdf.

Chapter 7

Office of Child Care, An Office of the Administration for Children & Families. "CCDF Reauthorization." Accessed January 5, 2016. http://www.acf.hhs.gov/programs/occ/ccdf-reauthorization.

United States Department of Education, "Building the Legacy: IDEA 2004. Developed in accordance with Section 508 of the U.S. Rehabilitation Act." Accessed January 5, 2016. http://idea.ed.gov.

Chapter 8

Espinosa, Linda M. "PreK-3rd: Challenging Common Myths About Young Dual Language Learners: An Update to the Seminal 2008 Report." New York: Foundation for Child Development, 2013.

Chapter 9

Aberson, Christopher L. and Sarah C. Haag. "Contact, Perspective Taking, and Anxiety as Predictors of Stereotype Endorsement, Explicit Attitudes, and Implicit Attitudes." *Group Processes & Intergroup Relations* 10(179) (2007).

Aberson, Christopher L., Carl Shoemaker, and Christina Tomolillo. "Implicit Bias and Contact: The Role of Interethnic Friendships." *Journal of Social Psychology* 144(335) (2004).

Antonio, Anthony L. "The Role of Interracial Interaction in the Development of Leadership Skills and Cultural Knowledge and Understanding." *Research in Higher Education* 42(593) (2001).

Beilock, Sian L., Allen R. McConnell, and Robert J. Rydell. "Stereotype Threat and Working Memory: Mechanisms, Alleviation, and Spillover." *Journal of Experimental Psychology: General* 136(256) (2007).

Benson, James and Geoffrey Borman. "Family, Neighborhood, and School Settings across Seasons: When Do Socioeconomic Context and Racial Composition Matter for the Reading Achievement Growth of Young Children?" *Teachers College Record* 112(1338) (2010).

Brown, Kathleen M. "The Educational Benefits of Diversity." *Leadership and Policy in Schools* 5(325) (2006).

Crisp, Richard and Rhiannon Turner. "Cognitive Adaptations to the Experience of Social and Cultural Diversity." *Psychological Bulletin* 137(242) (2011).

Denson, Nida. "Do Curricular and Co-curricular Diversity Activities Influence Racial Bias? A Meta-Analysis." *Review of Educational Research* 79(805) (2009).

Denson, Nida and Mitchell Chang. "Racial Diversity Matters: The Impact of Diversity-Related Student Engagement and Institutional Context." *American Educational Research Journal* 46(322) (2009).

Dovidio, John F., Samuel L. Gaertner, and Kerry Kawakami. "Implict and Explicit Prejudice and Interracial Interaction." *Journal of Personality & Social Psychology* 82(62) (2002).

Fisher v. University of Texas, 570 U.S. ___ (2013), Brief for Amici Curiae the College Board and the National School Board Association et al. in Support of Respondents. Filed August 13, 2012. (The NSBA represents over 13,800 elementary school districts.)

Fisher v. University of Texas, 570 U.S. ___ (2013), Brief of Amicus Curiae the American Psychological Association in Support of Respondents. Filed August 13, 2012.

Fisher v. University of Texas, 570 U.S. ___ (2013), Brief Amicus Curiae of the National Education Association et al., in Support of Respondents. Filed August 13, 2012.

Fisher v. University of Texas, 570 U.S. ___ (2013), Brief of Social and Organizational Psychologists as Amici Curiae Supporting Respondents. Filed August 13, 2012.

Mickelson, Roslyn A. "School Integration and K–12 Educational Outcomes: A Quick Synthesis of Social Science Evidence." *National Coalition on School Diversity Research Brief No. 5*, March 2015.

Mickelson, Roslyn Arlin and Martha Bottia. "Integrated Education and Mathematics Outcomes: A Synthesis of Social Science Research." *North Carolina Law Review* 88(993) (2010).

Nagda, Birenee A., Chan-woo Kim, and Yaffa Truelove. "Learning about Difference, Learning with Others, Learning to Transgress." *Journal of Social Issues* 60(195) (2004).

Pettigrew, Thomas F. and Linda R. Tropp. "How Does Intergroup Contact Reduce Prejudice? Meta-Analytic Tests of Three Mediators." *European Journal of Social Psychology* 38(922) (2008).

Reid, Jeanne L. and Sharon Lynn Kagan. "A Better Start: Why Classroom Diversity Matters in Early Education." The Century Foundation and the Poverty & Race Research Action Council, April 2015.

Saenz, Victor, Hoi Ning Ngai, and Sylvia Hurtado. "Factors Influencing Positive Interactions across Race for African American, Asian American, Latino and White College Students." *Research in Higher Education* 48(1) (2007).

Schmader, Toni, Chad E. Forbes, Shen Zhang, and Wendy Berry. "A Metacognitive Perspective on the Cognitive Deficits Experienced in Intellectually Threatening Environments." *Personality & Social Psychology Bulletin* 35(584) (2009).

Siegel-Hawley, Genevieve. "How Non-Minority Students Also Benefit from Racially Diverse Schools." *National Coalition on School Diversity Research Brief No. 8*, October 2012.

Sommers, Samuel R., Lindsey S. Warp, and Corrine C. Mahoney. "Cognitive Effects of Racial Diversity: White Individuals' Information Processing in Heterogeneous Groups." *Journal of Experimental Social Psychology* 44(1129) (2008).

Wood, Peter B. and Nancy Sonleitner. "The Effect of Childhood Interracial Contact on Adult Antiblack Prejudice." *International Journal of Intercultural Relations* 20(1) (1990).

Chapter 10

Ackerman, Debra J. and W. Steven Barnett. "Increasing the Effectiveness of Preschool Programs." *National Institute for Early Education Research* 11 (July 2006).

Association for Early Learning Leaders. Accessed on January 5, 2016. http://www.earlylearningleaders.org.

Child Care Aware. "Accreditation." Accessed on January 5, 2016. http://childcareaware.org/parents and guardians/parent information/accreditation.

Clifford, Richard M. and Stephanie S. Reszka. "Reliability and Validity of the Early Childhood Education Scale." Working Paper, FPG Child Development Institute, University of North Carolina at Chapel-Hill, January 2010.

Council for Professional Recognition. Accessed on January 5, 2016. http://www.cdacouncil.org.

Hestenes, Cassidy L., S. Mims, and S. Hestenes. "The North Carolina Rated License: A Three-Year Summary of Assessed Facilities, An Executive Summary 1999–2002." Greensboro, NC: University of North Carolina, 2003. http://ok.gov/sde/sites/ok.gov.sde/files/documents/files/PASS_PreK_OSDE.pdf.

Illinois Early Learning Project. "2013 Illinois Early Learning and Development Standards." Accessed on January 5, 2016. http://illinoisearlylearning.org/ields/.

Illinois State Board of Education. "Illinois Learning Standards: Social/Emotional Learning." Accessed January 5, 2016. http://www.isbe.net/ils/social_emotional/standards.htm.

Michigan State Board of Education. "Early Childhood Standards of Quality." Initially approved March 8, 2005; revised March 12, 2013. Accessed on January 5, 2016. http://www.michigan.gov/documents/mde/ECSQ_OK_Approved_422339_7.pdf.

National Association for the Education of Young Children. "NAEYC Early Childhood Program Standards and Accreditation Criteria & Guidance for Assessment." April 1, 2015. http://www.naeyc.org/files/academy/file/AllCriteriaDocument.pdf.

National Association for the Education of Young Children. "The 10 NAEYC Program Standards." Accessed on January 5, 2016. http://families.naeyc.org/accredited-article/10-naeyc-program-standards.

National Association for Family Child Care. Accessed on January 5, 2016. http://www.nafcc.org.

National Association for Family Child Care Foundation. "Getting Started in Self-Study: At-a-Glance." 2012. Accessed on January 5, 2016. http://www.nafcc.org/file/64b457e1-a2c6-4219-ba91-8a7b9d065000.

National Early Childhood Program Accreditation: National Accreditation Commission for Early Care and Education Programs. Accessed on January 5, 2016. http://www.necpa.net/index.php.

National Institute for Early Education Research. "The State of Preschool 2014: State Profile, Oklahoma." Accessed January 5, 2016. http://nieer.org/sites/nieer/files/Oklahoma_2014_0.pdf.

National Institute for Early Education Research. Accessed on January 5, 2016. http://www.nieer.org.

Office of Humanities and Early Childhood, Virginia Department of Education. "Virginia's Foundation Blocks for Early Learning: Comprehensive Standards for Four-Year-Olds." 2013. Accessed on January 5, 2016. http://www.doe.virginia.gov/instruction/early_childhood/preschool_initiative/foundationblocks.pdf.

Chapter 11

Barthe, Patte. "Starting Out Right." Center for Public Education, 2011.

Chapter 13

Hart, Betty and Todd R. Risley. *Meaningful Differences in the Everyday Experience of Young American Children*. Baltimore: Paul H. Brookes Publishing Company, 2003.

Katz, L. G. "What Should Young Children Be Doing?" *American Educator: The Professional Journal of the American Federation of Teachers* 12 (1988): 29–45.

McNamee, Gillian Dowley. *The High-Performing Preschool: Story Acting in Head Start Classrooms*. Chicago: The University of Chicago Press, 2015.

Chapter 14

Bodrova, Elena and Leong, Deborah. "Tools of the Mind: The Vygotskian Approach." In *Approaches to Early Childhood Education*, eds. Jaipaul L. Roopnarine and James E. Johnson. Boston: Pearson, 2013.

Fyfe, Brenda. "The Relationship between Documentation and Assessment." in *The Hundred Languages of Children*, eds. Carolyn Edwards, Lella Gandini, and George Forman. Santa Barbara: Praeger, 2012.

Gandini, Lella. "Reflections on Documentation." Transcription by Lynn White on file with authors at Loyola University Chicago School of Law, 25 E. Pearson, Chicago, Illinois 60611 (1996).

Harvard Graduate School of Education. "Project Zero: Making Learning Visible." Accessed January 5, 2016. http://www.pz.gse.harvard.edu/making_learning_visible.php.

Krechevsky, M., B. Mardell, M. Rivard, and D. Wilson. *Visible Learners: Promoting Reggio-Inspired Approaches in All Schools*. San Francisco: Jossey Bass, 2013.

Project Zero and Reggio Children. *Making Learning Visible: Children as Individual and Group Learners*. Reggio Emilia, Italy: Reggio Children, 2001.

Rinaldi, Carla. "The Pedagogy of Listening: The Listening Perspective from Reggio Emilia." In *The Hundred Languages of Children*, eds. C. Edwards, L. Gandini, and G. Foreman. Santa Barbara: Praeger, 2012.

Rinaldi, Carlina. "Observation and Documentation." Paper presented at Research Conference in Reggio, Emilia, Italy (June 1995), cited in Gunilla Dahlberg, "Pedagogical Documentation: A Practice for Negotiation and Democracy," in *The Hundred Languages of Children*, eds. C. Edwards, L. Gandini, and G. Foreman. Santa Barbara: Praeger, 2012.

Vygotsky, Lev. *Tool and Sign in the Development of the Child*. New York: Plenum Press, 1999.

Chapter 15

Dubner, Steven. "Does 'Early Education' Come Way Too Late? A New Freakonomics Radio Podcast." November 19, 2015. Accessed on January 5, 2016. http://freakonomics.com/2015/11/19/does-early-education-come-way-too-late-a-new-freakonomics-radio-podcast/.

Hart, Betty and Todd R. Risley. *Meaningful Differences in the Everyday Experience of Young American Children*. Baltimore: Paul H. Brookes Publishing Company, 2003.

Chapter 16

Harvard Graduate School of Education. "Project Zero: Making Learning Visible." Accessed January 5, 2016. http://www.pz.gse.harvard.edu/making_learning_visible.php.

Kaufman, Michael. "A Very Different Approach to Legal Education: The Reggio Emilia Method." *Endeavors* 4(12) (2014–2015).

Krechevsky, M., B. Mardell, M. Rivard, and D. Wilson. *Visible Learners: Promoting Reggio-Inspired Approaches in All Schools*. San Francisco: Jossey Bass, 2013.

Project Zero and Reggio Children. *Making Learning Visible: Children as Individual and Group Learners*. Reggio Emilia, Italy: Reggio Children, 2001.

Chapter 17

Chawla, L., K. Keena, I. Pevec, and E. Stanley. "Green Schoolyards as Havens from Stress and Resources for Resilience in Childhood and Adolescence." *Health Place* 28 (2014).

Krechevsky, Mara, Ben Mardell, and Angela N. Romans. "Engaging City Hall: Children as Citizens." *The New Educator* 10(1) (2014).

Louv, Richard. "'Sitting Is the New Smoking': What We Can Do About Killer Couches, Sedentary Schools, and the Pandemic of Inactivity." *Children & Nature Network*, March 2, 2013.

Merchant, Nilofer. "Sitting Is the Smoking of Our Generation." *Harvard Business Review*, January 14, 2013.

Rosen, Lawrence. "7 Science-Backed Reasons to Get Your Kids Outside." *Children & Nature Network*, October 14, 2015.

Chapter 18

Barnett, W. Steven, Megan E. Carolan, Jen Fitzgerald, and James H. Squires. *The State of Preschool 2012: State Preschool Yearbook*. New Brunswick, NJ: National Institute for Early Education Research, 2012.

Bellafante, Ginia. "Guiding Guided Play." *New York Times*, September 7, 2014.

Cadwell, Louise Boyd. *Bringing Reggio Emilia Home: An Innovative Approach to Early Childhood Education*. New York: Teachers College, Columbia University, 1997.

Campbell, F., E. Pungello, M. Burchinal, K. Kainz, Y. Pan, B. Wasik, O. Barbarin, J. Sparling, and C. Ramey. "Adult Outcomes as a Function of an Early Childhood Education Program: Abercedarian Project Follow Up," *Developmental Psychology* 48(4): July 2012.

Carey, Kevin. "The Funding Gap 2004: Many States Still Shortchange Low-Income and Minority Students." *The Education Trust*, Fall 2004.

Common Core of Data (CCD). "National Public Education Financial Survey: 2000–01 through 2010–11." *Digest of Education Statistics 2013*. Washington, DC: U.S. Department of Education, National Center for Education Statistics, December 2013.

Common Core of Data (CCD). "School District Finance Survey (F-33) FY 2009." Washington, DC: U.S. Department of Education, National Center for Education Statistics, 2009.

Costa, Kristina. "Fact Sheet: Social Impact Bonds in the United States." *Center for American Progress*, February 12, 2014.

Desmond, Conor. "Illinois's Future Is the Children: Why Funding Early Childhood Education Will Not Only Push Illinois' Economy to the Top But Will Play a Role in Paying Down Our Debt." *The Loyola University Chicago Journal of Early Education Law and Policy* (2014).

Education Week. "Calculating Social Impact Bonds." *Education Week*, August 12, 2013. Accessed January 5, 2016. http://www.edweek.org/ew/section/multimedia/social-impact-calculator.html.

Heckman, James J. "Invest in Early Childhood Development: Reduce Deficits, Strengthen the Economy." *Heckman*, December 7, 2014. Accessed January 5, 2016. http://heckmanequation.org/content/resource/invest-early-childhood-development-reduce-deficits-strengthen-economy.

Heckman, James J. "Letter to National Commission on Fiscal Responsibility and Budget Reform." *Heckman*. Accessed on January 5, 2016. http://heckmanequation.org/content/resource/letter-national-commission-fiscal-responsibility-and-reform.

Heckman, James J. "Schools, Skills, and Synapses." *Economic Inquiry* 46 (2008).

Heckman, James J., Seong Hyeok Moon, Rodrigo Pinto, Peter A. Savelyev, and Adam Yavitz. "The Rate of Return to the HighScope Perry Preschool Program." *Journal of Public Economics* 94 (2010).

Heckman, James J., Seong Hyeok Moon, Rodrigo Pinto, Peter Savelyev, and Adam Yavitz. "A Reanalysis of the HighScope Perry Preschool Program." University of Chicago, April 24, 2009.

Heckman, James J., Rodrigo Pinto, and Peter Savelyev. "Understanding the Mechanisms through Which an Influential Early Childhood Program Boosted Adult Outcomes." *American Economic Review* 103(6) (2013): 2052–86.

Hussar, William J. and Tabitha M. Bailey. *Projections of Education Statistics to 2021.* Washington, DC: U.S. Department of Education National Center for Education Statistics, January 2013.

Kaufman, Michael J. and Sherelyn R. Kaufman. *Education Law, Policy and Practice: Cases and Materials.* New York: Wolters Kluwer, 2013.

The Learning Curve. Accessed on January 5, 2016. http://thelearningcurve.pearson.com.

Lu, Adrienne. "Elected Officials Embrace Preschool, But Funding Is the Catch." *The Pew Charitable Trusts*, February 28, 2014.

National Center for Education Statistics. "Digest of Education Statistics: Table 205." Washington, DC: U.S. Department of Education National Center for Education Statistics, 2013.

National Center for Education Statistics. "Fast Facts." Washington, DC: U.S. Department of Education National Center for Education Statistics, 2014.

National School Board Association. "Unfunded Mandates Frustrate Superintendents and Principals." *National School Boards Association School Board News*, November 25, 2003.

New America Foundation, U.S. Departments of Education, Health & Human Services, Agriculture, Defense, and Veterans Affairs, White House Office of Management and Budget, and Congressional Budget Office. *The Federal Education Budget.* New America Foundation Federal Budget Project, 2014.

Sahlberg, Pasi and Paul Michael Garcia. *Finnish Lessons: What Can the World Learn from Educational Change in Finland?* New York: Teachers College Press, 2012.

San Antonio Independent School Dist. v. Rodriguez, 411 U.S. 1, 49-53 (1973).

Schweinhart, Lawrence J., Jeanne Montie, Zongping Xiang, W. Steven Barnett, Clive R. Belfield, and Milagros Nores. *Lifetime Effects: The HighScope Perry Preschool Study Through Age 40.* Ypsilanti: HighScope Press, 2005.

Schweinhart, Lawrence J. and David P. Weikart. "The HighScope Model of Early Childhood Education." In *Approaches to Early Childhood Education*, eds. Jaipaul L. Roopnarine and James E. Johnson. Boston: Pearson, 2013.

Senate Committee on Health, Education, Labor and Pensions. "The Every Child Achieves Act of 2015." Accessed January 5, 2016. http://www.help.senate.gov/imo/media/The_Every_Child_Achieves_Act_of_2015--summary.pdf.

Snyder, Thomas D. and Sally A. Dillow. *Digest of Education Statistics 2012.* Washington, DC: U.S. Department of Education National Center for Education Statistics, December 2013.

Social Finance. "International Development: What If You Could Invest in Development?" *Social Finance Ltd.* Accessed January 5, 2016. http://www.socialfinance.org.uk/work/developmentimpactbonds.

U.S. Department of Education. "Early Learning: America's Middle Class Promise Begins Early." Accessed on January 5, 2016. http://www.ed.gov/early-learning.

About the Authors

Sherelyn R. Kaufman, JD, MAT, has practiced education law at private firms and the U.S. Department of Education's Office for Civil Rights, and has taught, advised, and directed early childhood education programs. She now serves as a member of the Adjunct Faculty at the Erikson Institute Graduate School of Child Development. She is the author of leading peer-reviewed articles regarding the school-family relationship, and is the coauthor with Elizabeth Nelson and Michael Kaufman of *Learning Together: The Law, Politics, Economics, Pedagogy, and Neuroscience of Early Childhood Education* (2015).

Michael J. Kaufman, JD, MA, is the Interim Dean, professor of law, and director of the Education Law and Policy Institute at Loyola University Chicago School of Law. He is the author and coauthor of countless books and articles in the field of education policy, including the leading education law and policy textbook used in law schools and graduate schools, *Education Law, Policy and Practice*, 3rd Edition (2013), and most recently *Learning Together: The Law, Politics, Economics, Pedagogy, and Neuroscience of Early Childhood Education* (2015).

Elizabeth C. Nelson, JD, MAT, taught third grade in the city of Chicago, practiced law in the Office of the Attorney General for the State of Illinois, and is a professor on the Adjunct Faculty at Loyola University Chicago School of Law. She is the coauthor of *Learning Together* as well as articles regarding education policy and pedagogy.